A Different Accent

Michael Henderson

GROSVENOR BOOKS USA

Published By
GROSVENOR BOOKS USA
15 Rio Vista Lane, Richmond, Virginia 23226

Also available from

GROSVENOR BOOKS
54 Lyford Road
London SW18 3JJ
England

GROSVENOR BOOKS
21 Dorcas Street
South Melbourne, Victoria 3205
Australia

GROSVENOR BOOKS
PO Box 1834
Wellington,
New Zealand

ISBN 0 901269 90 5
© Michael Henderson 1985
Printed in the United States of America
by Dynagraphics, Inc., Portland, Oregon

A Different Accent

By the same author
FROM INDIA WITH HOPE
EXPERIMENT WITH UNTRUTH

to Juliet

Contents

Foreword

by Clay Myers

THE DIFFERENT ACCENT is English. The perspective, however, is universal. In this collection of talks Michael Henderson speaks to Americans and, indeed, to all people in a language that is clear, readable and sometimes a little disconcerting.

From de Tocqueville to Henderson, Americans swallow hard under examination by outsiders, then appreciate the insights.

Mr. Henderson's pen is a sword that cuts many ways, illuminating several sides of issues people feel deeply about. As he says, he wants to enlarge horizons, to create a global outlook and thereby to change the way we think and live.

Henderson is now living in Oregon, a state that is proud of its environmental livability. This book promotes the *human* livability. The common thread throughout urges greater tolerance and understanding of those from a different race or culture or political viewpoint. Along the way the reader is introduced to fascinating people from other nations. Henderson's goal is to reduce the *we* versus *they* syndrome. He succeeds.

In his life as in his talks, Mr. Henderson seeks to explain our differences, looking constantly for the silver lining of common goals and causes and with hope for the future reconciliation of history's past enemies.

Still an Englishman, Henderson makes clear his admiration for the principles and the freedoms expressed in the Declaration of Independence. Thankful for such a heritage, the author's view of America is as a nurturing place for global understandings.

In one of the talks Henderson quotes the final statement of the Oregon Code of Ethics of Journalism: "We affirm the printed word, medium of global communication, is a means to the end of freeing the human mind from bigotry, hate and intolerance, and

Clay Myers, from a pioneer Oregon family, served in Oregon state government for nineteen years. A former Oregon Secretary of State and also State Treasurer, he is now in investment counseling in New York.

for the establishment of better living, international peace and justice to all."

I have been privileged to know this gifted, dedicated couple, Michael and his wife, Erica, as they carry out the important purpose of their lives. The reader is welcomed to the same appreciation through this book.

1 Seasons

Fourth of July

YESTERDAY was the 4th of July. Those who listen to me regularly will know that I have a love affair with the United States, that I'm grateful for its past, respectful of its present and full of hope for what it will mean in the future. So today I'd like to look beyond the fireworks and the parties to what yesterday represents for the world.

As a small English boy during World War II I grew up in this country, in New England, so rich in American heritage. Bunker Hill was as familiar to me as the Battle of Hastings, Concord Bridge caught my imagination more than London Bridge. I could recite the presidents of the United States not the kings of England. John Paul Jones was not a pirate, as I am sure he is depicted in our history books, but a hero. I even played the part of Nathan Hale in my school play. Before entering my teens and returning to England I was familiar with the Preamble to the Declaration of Independence: "We hold these truths to be self-evident, that all men are created equal; that they are endowed by their Creator with certain inalienable rights, that among these are life, liberty and the pursuit of happiness."

I imbibed all these experiences and sentiments without in any way diminishing my pride in my own country. I was there in the crowd, a proud little English boy, when Churchill spoke in Harvard Yard during the war. Even at the time of the birth of the United States many Englishmen, of course, could see beyond the immediate struggle. Lord Chatham, the former Prime Minister Pitt, speaking in the House of Lords about the Philadelphia Congress, said, "When your Lordships consider their decency, firmness and wisdom you cannot but respect their cause and wish to make it your own. For solidity of reasoning, force of sagacity and wisdom of conclusion, no body of men can stand in preference to the General Congress of Philadelphia and all attempts to impose servitude upon such a mighty continental nation must be in vain."

Many English men and women thrilled to what was a declaration of independence from Britain because it represented then and still does a step forward for mankind. As Abraham Lincoln said years later, "The sentiment in the Declaration of Independence gave not only liberty to the people of this country but hope to all the world for all future time."

The American revolution was achieved with few of the bloody excesses associated with so many revolutions. It established freedom not its subversion as so many revolutions have. It is inseparable from the leadership of men like Washington, Jefferson, the two Adams, Madison, Hamilton, Franklin. It was also a product of teamwork at the top. The Declaration, though drafted by Jefferson, was the work of a team with an overall review by Congress. As Franklin said to Hancock, "We must all hang together or we shall most assuredly hang separately."

The revolution succeeded because of the courage and sacrifice of men and women who pledged lives, fortunes and sacred honor. We are all familiar with Patrick Henry's, "Give me liberty or give me death." But how about this from Abigail Adams. Asked whether if she had known that her husband was going to have stayed so long abroad she would have consented to it, she said, "If I had known, Sir, that Mr. Adams could have effected what he has done, I would not only have submitted to the absence I have endured, painful as it has been, but I would not have opposed it even though three more years should be added to the number, which Heaven avert. I feel a pleasure in being able to sacrifice my selfish passions to the general good, and in imitating the example which has taught me to consider myself and family but as the small dust of the balance when compared with the great community."

The political philosophy of those at the heart of the revolution stemmed from the acceptance of a universal moral law which they believed to be the expression of God's authority in the affairs of the world. "For the hope of public virtue must be frustrated if individuals be not influenced by moral principle," the Senate told George Washington at his first inauguration. Washington defined the whole duty of life as "obedience to God's will."

American independence meant the cutting off of the shackles

of the past and the creation of a sovereign nation. But it was more than that. Historian Samuel Eliot Morison says that if the American revolution had produced nothing more than the Declaration of Independence it would have been worthwhile. "The beauty and cogency of the Preamble, reaching back to remotest antiquity and forward to an indefinite future," he wrote, "have lifted the hearts of millions of men and will continue to do so. These words are more revolutionary than anything written by Robespierre, Marx or Lenin, more explosive than the atom, a continual challenge to ourselves as well as an inspiration to the oppressed of all the world."

"Wherever we have been faithful to this trust the world has benefited," writes Francis Bradley in *The American Proposition* from which I have culled this historical material. "Where we have been faithless the world has suffered."

Will we rise to a prediction once made by Jefferson: "Our children will be as wise as we are and will establish in the fullness of time those things not yet ripe for establishment."

Just a footnote: Adams and Jefferson who had together fathered the Declaration of Independence both lived on for fifty years and died on the same day in 1826. It was the 4th of July. Believe it — or not!

July 5, 1984

Thanksgiving I

SOME AMERICANS seem ready to believe the worst about their government, to impugn the motives of the military and to give this country's foes the benefit of every doubt.

Others have an unshakeable belief in the superiority of the American way of life, extol the "magic of the marketplace" and would agree with those Grants Pass constituents who think there's nothing wrong with the United Nations except all those foreigners.

One lot constantly underestimates the hope of freedom that this country still represents to millions of people in the world. They might benefit from an extended stay in a country where they were muzzled.

The other lot somehow ascribe to themselves some inherent natural virtue and fail to see where the real credit belongs. They remind me of the time my daughter, then four, watched a magician on television. With a flourish he produced out of nowhere a wriggling guinea pig. "Oh," said my daughter, "what a clever guinea pig!"

Thanksgiving is a time when most Americans will want to honor the master magician. As the first Thanksgiving proclamation stated 120 years ago, "No human counsel hath devised nor hath any mortal hand worked out these great things. They are the gracious gifts of the Most High God."

Thanksgiving is a time, too, when those of us who are not Americans might be permitted to express a word of thanks to this country.

Recently the bands of Britain's Black Watch and Scots Guards regiments gave a display in the Portland Coliseum. In the course of their program they played a musical tribute to the United States armed forces. When they launched into the stirring strains of *Semper fidelis* the whole audience was quickly on its feet.

I was grateful for this British gesture of appreciation to America. One of the hardest things in these days, and in recent years, for those whose relatives died in the service of their country must be to feel that their sacrifice was unappreciated, even in some cases resented.

History has laid heavy world burdens on America's shoulders. She dare not shrink from them. But too often America receives not appreciation but spattered paint, not bouquets but bullets. Yet we in Europe owe our very existence to the sacrifice of American lives, our recovery after World War II to the most generous aid plan in history, and our future to the defensive guarantees offered by this land.

Unfortunately this apparent lack of gratitude adds to the self-doubt of Americans who are beginning to wonder whether the values in their own society are worth propagating or defending.

I was talking this week with a lady recently arrived in Portland from Poland. I asked her why she had come. All her life, she said, she had dreamed that one day she might live in freedom. It was hard, she told me, for those who had never lost their freedom to appreciate what that meant. We take so much for granted.

We do not realize how remarkably open American government is. The way, for instance, the abilities and beliefs of appointees and their suitability for public office are probed before the TV cameras, the way the processes by which policies are arrived at are exposed and dissected. In no place in the world does freedom of the press enjoy such protection—consider the uproar over the government's decision to exclude journalists from accompanying a rescue or invasion fleet, or the way in which a deliberately fear-provoking film invades our homes without invitation. In few countries is so much energy, thought and money put into helping minorities have access to what others have, from wheelchair legislation to equal employment practices. As the Secretary of State in Peter Howard's satirical musical, *The Vanishing Island*, boasts to the Communists,

> But we've freedom to spy in the press,
> We are free in our homes to raise hell there.
> Politicians can get in a mess
> Without being purged for their welfare.

But politicians can be replaced. That is the bottom line which really distinguishes democracy from dictatorship. We may as individuals be no more moral than people who live under another system. But the ultimate test of how free our society is, how far we may trust our leaders, is that they submit to the ballot with regularity. We should never forget that great divide.

Of course America has made mistakes, there are many abuses at home and abroad. There is a long way to go before we create the ideal society, as Minoru Yasui said speaking to the Portland City Club this past week. He was one of thousands of US citizens of Japanese ancestry who was interned during World War II. He is seeking redress for his own conviction for violating a curfew at that time. But he seeks redress, as he said, because he believes in America, because he believes that this is a land where ultimately justice must prevail, where individual dignity is recognized.

Despite his sad experiences forty years ago, he affirmed in

ringing terms, "This is the greatest country in the world. Let's make it even greater. It is the hope of mankind."

That is surely the right sort of patriotism, honesty about one's country's faults but faith that they can be corrected and a decision to do something about them. That sort of America will win the world.

An Australian journalist, Gordon Wise, spoke at a conference in Washington, DC this week on the leadership the world looked to from America, and the tasks democratic nations must shoulder together. We had to be willing, he said, to defend what we believed in from the attacks of those who ruthlessly sought to run the world their way. But adequate defense had to include a commitment to live out and offer a better way. True love of country did not lead to looking down on others. It meant expressing the best interests of one's own country in such a way that other countries were not left out but felt that we were concerned for their best interests also.

"Convinced of our own ideology," he said, "the democracies could seek to involve what are now conceived as our enemies in a change process which includes bettering, not threatening mankind."

Such an involvement would be a real cause for Thanksgiving.

November 24, 1983

Thanksgiving II

A LITTLE AMERICAN GIRL lived in England for the first four years of her life. When she came back to America recently she was quite astonished when she was told that America didn't have a queen. "But," she said, in an observation only a child could make, "if they don't have a queen, who's on their pound notes?"

There's a lot about America for foreigners, too, to learn. And of course a little learning can be a dangerous thing. I remember meeting a Virginian in Paris. He told me that his family came to America in the 1600's. In my knowledgeable way I murmured something about the Mayflower. He quickly put me in my place. "Oh, no," he said, "we had our own ship."

I saw in the papers this week that there was a certain controversy in Australia about the celebration of the country's bicentennial as many of their original ships brought convicts. I often think in that connection of the little Australian girl who was told that as a treat she was going to England. She burst into tears. "What's the matter?" her mother asked. "I don't want to go to England," she cried. "That's where all the convicts come from."

That's a different perspective. And sometimes I think Americans are in need these days of a different perspective about their country. I have noticed that they are prone to dwell more on the country's faults and mistakes than on its achievements and strengths, to be more aware of foreign criticisms than foreign appreciation. It's a pity that there isn't a world Thanksgiving Day for America.

Some months back I heard the Nigerian Ambassador to the United States speak in Portland. What was his theme? What Nigeria can learn from America. As a small boy, he said, he had learned the American Declaration of Independence by heart. His people drew inspiration from Abraham Lincoln. "This is a country of noble thoughts," he said.

A short time ago I heard the Kenyan Ambassador to this country speak in Portland. What did he say? "We envy you and we look up to you when creating our institutions, the fact that you have chosen democracy." He spoke of a photograph in *Newsweek* he had seen which more than anything else epitomized for him the strength of America. It was at the time of Sadat's death and four U.S. Presidents were pictured together. In few other countries in the world could that happen, he said. In many lands former presidents would either have been killed or be in hiding in the bush. He was so struck by the photo that he had written to *Newsweek* for a copy.

Similarly I heard a senior Pakistani speak in Portland last week. "If you have a world calamity," he said, "it is this country which sends help."

Naturally all these gentlemen are not unaware of aspects of this country's policies with which they are not satisfied. But because they value freedom, and we sometimes take its benefits for granted, they have that larger perspective.

Mihajlo Mihajlov, a brave and perceptive Yugoslav dissident who has spent many years in prison, refers to the United States as "a country that is still like a fairy-tale land and was founded by those who place freedom of conscience above all other narrow, self-serving interests." He writes, "America continues to be the homeland for all the people on our earth because a person's real homeland is freedom. The time will come when the U.S. will defend freedom throughout the world, just as other states defend their subjects."

It is not that Americans should be starry-eyed about the country. As a challenging essay in *Time* magazine stated nearly fifteen years ago, "It can be argued that only the nation that has faced up to its own failings and acknowledged its capacities for evil and ill-doing has any real claim to greatness." The original Thanksgiving was not a time when the Pilgrims were thanking God for their own virtues. Rather they were recognizing the way some outside force had protected them from harm.

The English author J.B. Priestley once wrote, "We should behave toward our country as women behave toward the men they love. A loving wife will do anything for her husband except to stop criticizing and trying to improve him. That is the right attitude for a citizen. We should cast the same affectionate but sharp glance at our country. We should love it, but also insist on telling it all its faults."

Two visions of America compete, according to Rodney Page, Executive Director of Ecumenical Ministries of Oregon, speaking at the Hilton last week. Those who see the country as a vast storehouse to be plundered, where compassion is weakness, competition reigns, the least government is best and the fittest survive. And those who see America as a land of plenty and have been willing to share her treasure with the whole inhabited earth. This second vision has been like a magnet, he said, pulling away from the chain gangs, the lynch mobs and the sweat shops, where a compassionate people sees government assisting those least able to help themselves.

This Thanksgiving I as an Englishman will be giving thanks for that kind of compassionate America. My gratitude goes way back. As a small boy I was evacuated to America during World War II and adopted for five years by a family completely unknown to my brother and me who looked after us as if we were their own. That is the kind of generosity for which Americans are known. Criticism of America is often a reflection of the great expectations other people have of this country. This Thanksgiving, this family time, perhaps Americans could pause and give thought to the whole world family, most of whom have never eaten the kind of meal we will be enjoying and never will unless we in the Western nations voluntarily decide to accept larger aims and greater restraints in our own lives.

Let us not take the advice of a cartoon in *The New Yorker.* A man is seen reaching for another helping. The caption reads, "More please. Americans overeat and, by God, I'm an American."

November 25, 1982

Christmas

AT THIS SEASON of the year we talk about three wise men from the East who lived two thousand years ago. I would like to spend a little time on three wise people from the East today.

If I were to ask any reasonably well informed Americans to compile lists of the greatest figures alive chances are that these three names would appear on most lists and that after these three it would be difficult to find consensus.

One is Albanian, from a peasant family in Yugoslavia, now at home in a slum in India. One is Polish, son of an army officer, dwelling in a palace in Italy. One is Russian, a former Marxist-Leninist, from a family persecuted for being Czarists, living in the woods of Vermont. All three were born in that turbulent decade which produced World War I. All three are Christian. I refer to Mother Teresa, Pope John Paul 2 and Alexander Solzhenitsyn.

If suffering and sacrifice are the crucible which forges prophets they have all served their apprenticeship. Mother Teresa, a

Roman Catholic nun, requested permission from the Superior of her Order, the Loreto Sisters in India, to leave the protected cloister where she taught in order to work in the slums of Calcutta. It was, she said, a call within a call to the poorest of the poor. Since her modest beginning, with five rupees in her purse, the Missionaries of Charity have caught the imagination of the world. The latest sight we had of her was as she moved compassionately among the sufferers in Bhopal.

Pope John Paul 2, soccer player, canoeist, skier, theological professor, whose first love was theater and dance, has survived two near fatal traffic accidents. He had to go underground during the Nazi occupation of his country, rescuing Jewish families from execution, and working in a stone quarry to escape arrest at a time when 3000 priests lost their lives in concentration camps. He became a Bishop under the Communist regime.

And Alexander Solzhenitsyn, who served as an artillery officer in World War II, for criticizing Stalin spent eight years in the *Gulag Archipelago* about which he has written so powerfully. He also overcame cancer. After exile in his own country he was banished abroad.

The views of this trio are not fashionable. They are often a challenge to conventional thinking. Despite his years in a Soviet prison Solzhenitsyn says that the dividing line between good and evil does not run between countries or political parties or ideologies but through the heart of every individual. He sees the willpower of the well off being sapped by what he calls the spirit of Munich, "the everyday state of those who have given in to the desire for well-being at any price."

The Pope has not let an attempt on his life prevent him from reaching out to the world. Most of us will remember that picture of him a year ago as he sat with his would-be assassin. "I spoke to him as a brother whom I have pardoned," said His Holiness. It was reminiscent of years before when he was one of the Polish bishops who reached out a hand of reconciliation to the bishops of Germany.

And Mother Teresa has a simplicity and directness in her care for the dying as in her dealing with Western sophisticates. I have seen a TV inquisitor so taken aback by her straightness that he had to be helped from the screen. "Being unwanted, being lonely," she has told Western audiences, "this poverty is much harder to alleviate than the poverty of hungry people. If we are lonely or full of hate, a plate of rice is not going to satisfy."

I have a feeling that if all three ever met together they would find, despite their different formations, an extraordinary amount in common. It would be enough to make the devil tremble! I would love to eavesdrop on a conversation between them. In all three an unshakeable commitment to unwavering principle is tempered by a warm out-going personality.

Pope John Paul 2, the first non-Italian Pope in 415 years, the youngest for 130 years, is a symbol of hope to millions of believers in Eastern Europe. Said a Pole when he was elected Pope, "He was our friend but now he has gone to be the friend of the whole world." An English bishop commented after the Pope's visit to his country, "Because God is so real to him, he makes it easier for those who meet him to believe in God."

Alexander Solzhenitsyn, the greatest Russian writer since Tolstoy, is laboring to resurrect the buried history of his people in this century. He believes that his country and the world have gone their disastrous ways because "men have forgotten God." Our lives, he maintains, should consist "not in the pursuit of material success but in the quest of worthy spiritual growth."

And the humble approach of Mother Teresa who calls herself "a little pencil in the hand of God" is well summed up in a reply she gave to a friend of mine who asked her if she wasn't worried what would happen to her work after she had gone. "No," she said. "I'm sure someone more helpless will come along."

What a remarkable thing that three such unique personalities, who feel called not to reflect the world's wisdom but to change it, should have been exported to the world from Eastern Europe. They, like the wise men of old, are followers of a star.

December 20, 1984

New Year

I WANT TODAY to look back over the year at what might be called silver linings. They are encouraging events one can set against the dark clouds of tragedies like the assassination of Mrs. Gandhi and the Bhopal gas leak, the starvation in Ethiopia and other African countries, and the American deaths in Beirut. We may have overlooked some with our election fixation.

Last year I said that I hoped that 1984 would be a year of faith rather than fear. I little thought that I would be able to characterize it as a year of forgiveness.

The year began with a *Time* cover story on the Pope's act of forgiving his would-be assassin. "A pardon from the Pontiff, a lesson in forgiveness for a troubled world," was the magazine article's subhead. The Pope was behind the scenes, too, in the ending this year of a century of conflict between Argentina and Chile over the Beagle Channel, a conflict that nearly led to war in 1979. Under the terms of the Vatican-mediated settlement, Chile has been awarded sovereignty over three main disputed islands but Argentina retains maritime rights to the surrounding waters. The Chilean foreign minister called the treaty "a just, equitable and honorable solution." The Argentine foreign minister said the pact "constitutes an example not only for the people of our region but also for the world."

There was another reconciliation in the visit to Tokyo of South Korean President Chun Doo Hwan to end, as he said, "the unfortunate past shared by our two countries." Welcoming the President, the Emperor of Japan said, "It is indeed regrettable that there has existed an unfortunate past between us for a period in this century and I believe it should not be repeated." The London *Times* headlined its report, "Hirohito ends 400 years of bitterness." Prime Minister Nakasone, referring to great sufferings inflicted on Koreans, added, "I would like to state here that the government and people of Japan feel a deep regret for this error."

A remarkable photo underlined yet another reconciliation which we take for granted on the other side of the world. It was of President François Mitterand of France and Chancellor Helmut

Kohl of Germany holding hands while their national anthems were played at Verdun, scene of one of the most bitter battles between the two nations in World War I.

I think of three similar events. One was the signing of the treaty with Hong Kong between China and Britain. It may, as *The Christian Science Monitor* headlined, "be set in ink." It is a venture with risk. But it shows, as Prime Minister Thatcher said, how the most intractable problems can be solved peacefully. Another was the peaceful agreement between Britain and Spain over the re-opening of Gibraltar's border with Spain. It had been sealed in 1969 when Franco hoped to starve the people of "the rock." Even in 1981 the Spanish king refused to attend the wedding of Prince Charles and Lady Diana because the couple were visiting Gibraltar on their honeymoon. And thirdly there was the brave overture of President Duarte of El Salvador to the rebels at Las Palmas, risking retribution from far right and left.

The Bhopal disaster and the Gandhi assassination had silver linings. As Mother Teresa said at Bhopal, "It has brought out the best in everybody. This has got these people to share, to serve the suffering, who would never have become involved otherwise." Experts rate the medical response as outstanding. It was, as *The New York Times* commented, "a fast, intelligent, comprehensive marshalling of manpower, supplies and equipment to meet a need that at first seemed desperate beyond belief." Lives were saved and total impairment prevented, and many Westerners wondered whether their sophisticated society would have done as well.

On the killing of Sikhs, I noted an article by Indian journalist Prem Shanker Jha, in which he described the courageous way Hindus had protected Sikhs. It had been an awesome humbling experience, he wrote, to see the way the nation came together after despair. "I do not know whether the damage done by the assassination and the rioting against Sikhs that followed can ever be wholly undone. But I do know that the healing process that has already begun could only have taken place in a democracy, and a strong and vibrant one at that."

I also noted that India sent 100,000 tons of grain to alleviate the famine in Africa. In several articles I saw India's self-sufficiency in food production held up as an example for Africa.

The tragedy in Ethiopia also brought out the best in people. An AP story reported that "the Americans and Soviets, in one of their major emergency-response efforts since World War II are putting aside their countries differences to work together on the airlift taking food and supplies to millions of starving Ethiopian famine victims."

It brought our community together, too. I was at Portland airport to see the loading of 47 tons of wheat and medical supplies for the stricken country. A fund drive which began with an offer by the US Bank of a matching gift of $50,000, has brought in nearly $600,000. Pendleton Flour Mill provided the wheat at cost and milled and transported it to Portland free of charge. And Evergreen International Airlines flew it to Ethiopia, the equivalent of a gift of a quarter million dollars. John Banda, from US Bank, himself from Malawi, told me, "It has been so moving to have the city respond to a place so far. It is an outpouring of sympathy and dollars."

One last silver lining. While some other UN agencies are getting adverse publicity UNICEF announces that the lives of half a million children were saved in 1984 by using a simple, inexpensive method to combat dehydration, the single biggest cause of death among third world infants.

December 27, 1984

2 Role of the press

Why I write

I WAS INTERVIEWED by a journalist last week who asked me, "What is your philosophy of writing?" I was a bit taken aback. I suppose I shouldn't have been. I had just never been asked it like that before, never really taken time to think out why I write what I write. I had taken my writing philosophy for granted, seen it simply as an extension of how I lived and what I lived for.

Regular listeners to my weekly commentaries will, I guess, have formed some impressions of my attitudes. Those, at least, who have got beyond the novelty of my accent. It's funny but in conversations here I get the distinct impression that some people are listening not to what I say but to the way I say it. I opened my mouth at a party the other day and a lady said to me, "Were you born in a foreign country?" "No," I replied quite truthfully, "I was born in England."

That journalist's question to me last week, however, has caused me to consider the why of my commentaries. Basically, I write and speak to change the way people live and think. I write to share insights and lessons, and attitudes, and hopes I have gleaned as the fruit of contact with very fine men and women all over the world, many of them associated with the program of Moral Re-Armament.

Two usual motives for a writer — ambition and money — are not fundamentally mine. Though occasionally, of course, they may rear their tempting heads. It's nice to hear your books or articles or speeches praised or quoted. It's nice to receive the occasional unexpected larger check. It's disappointing when something you have sweated over and thought was good gets rejected by someone you quickly assume is lacking in judgement. My last book was turned down by forty publishers before it was accepted.

One motive I have is to enlarge horizons. In this dangerous age in which we live it is vital to be knowledgeable about other countries and what motivates their peoples. We are, whether we like it or not, interdependent. What is in the world interest is in our national interest, though we don't always realize it.

Sometimes we think that we are the center of the world. The English have this failing though on a lesser scale than we used to. There was once a headline in an English newspaper which read, "Fog in the channel, continent isolated." Sometimes, too, we are tempted to think that we have a monopoly on sensible attitudes, that we are the sane ones. What about that absurd slogan which one of our local TV news teams adopted last year: "There really is a crazy world out there." I'm glad that didn't last long. A Scots friend of mine recently retired to his home in Scotland. He didn't take kindly to the suggestion of one of his English friends that he might find it difficult to live so far from anywhere. I'd like to contribute to the creation of a global perspective.

It is so easy to fall into the prevailing mood about other countries, to judge them superficially, to let media shorthand about them and their leaders condition our responses. So I'd like to add to the balance of our knowledge of the world, also to help everyone realize that there are a lot more hopeful things going on than might be apparent from the headlines. A diet of gloomy news produces consumers like the man who wrote to *Readers Digest:* "Dear Sir. I have read your powerful article on the dangers of smoking and as a result I have decided to give up reading." I suppose that I do not get as depressed as some because I know of people all round the world who are working without bias and without blame for reconciliation and justice. I hope in future commentaries to tell you more about them.

There are so many ways in which society gets polarized and I would like to work for a greater tolerance and understanding of those who differ from us. I would like in my writing to reduce the *us* and *them* syndrome. In the peace movement people who should be working together are at odds. Arab and Jew, Catholic and Protestant, black and white, rich and poor, so many divisions have to bridged, so many wrongs have to be righted. And there are not enough who recognize the truth that when I point my finger at my neighbor there are three more pointing back at me. How quickly we judge ourselves by our ideals and others by their actions.

In the past eighteen months I have talked about some of the people who have been an encouragement because they have demonstrated that a different way is possible as they started with themselves: the Australian politician who gave up his self-centered ambition and has worked, in office and out, to enhance the dignity of the Aborigine people; the white Kenyan whose father was buried alive by the Mau Mau and is a catalyst for racial harmony on the continent; the Brazilian trade unionist who was reconciled with a rival trade unionist who had vowed to kill him and helped end gangsterism in his port; the Norwegian who read the fine print in a competition's rules and forfeited the chance to win a large sum of money and whose integrity has won the trust of Soviet dissidents. They have underlined for us the need for an answer in the world to start with the discipline we accept in our own lives. They have shown that everyone can change, that what we say and do can make the difference between changing others or freezing them in their attitudes. As Peter Howard, the English journalist to whom I owe most of what I know about writing, said about his own work, "I write to encourage men to accept the growth in character that is essential if civilization is to survive."

Let me end with a cartoon which I once saw in the English humor magazine *Punch*. A minister was standing in the pulpit in church obviously delivering a sermon. The caption was his words to the congregation: "If your lifestyle is going to be seriously affected then of course disregard everything I've said."

January 20, 1983

The character of journalists

I WAS ONCE ASKED to cover an international conference abroad. It seemed to be going well. But obviously the British journalists, because they had been so briefed or more likely because of an innate sense of what is accepted as news in Britain, were probing for and accentuating any areas of division. Some of this was reflected in their choice of words. "Mr. Heath reacted angrily" when they might have written "The British Prime Minister spoke firmly." It was interesting that the German journalists were approaching the subject less combatively. The result was that one of my German colleagues found himself phoned up by his editor and asked why he was not reporting the imminent breakup of the conference as predicted in that morning's British papers. Well, as it happened there was no breakup and, because the conference was successful, not much news either.

But the experience showed me that perceptions of such an event are shaped by the training and motives of those reporting it and their editors. Mort Rosenblum in his book *Coups and Earthquakes* says that because of competition for space correspondents tend to squeeze the last drop out of stories they cover. This leads to a malpractice known as hyping. "Few exaggerate purposely," he writes, "and almost none ever lies outright." But reporters are often tempted to reach for dramatic conclusions or wide generalizations to make their stories more attractive to editors. Occasionally quotes are, as he calls it, "cleaned up" slightly to sound catchier. In borderline cases stronger words are usually preferred. "Riot" instead of "demonstration," "massacre" instead of "killings." "These factors," he claims, "aggravate the average person's natural tendency to see more than is really there."

I know that some years back when my mother was living in what was then Rhodesia, the *Daily Express* in London had a frightening story about killings in Salisbury. It gave a sense that those living in the capital were in danger. I phoned my mother and discovered that she had not heard anything about them.

Of course, the moment anyone suggests correcting anything in the press there are cries of censorship. The press is a lot slower at owning up to its own shortcomings than about protesting any encroachment on its freedom. George Will wrote in *Newsweek* once, "The public confidence in journalists is jeopardized by these overwrought reactions to every small limit on their expansive privileges."

One of our principal investigative newspapers in Britain, the *Sunday Times,* some years back had playwright Arnold Wesker spend seven weeks in its offices with a view to capturing what it was like on such a paper. When it came time to print his article the paper suppressed it. As Derek Ingram, head of the respected agency Gemini, writes, "Journalists should not be oversensitive to examination of their performance by lay people. We are, after all, always only too ready to examine everyone else's business."

Any worthwhile changes that come to the media in a democracy are not going to be imposed from without by legislation but by voluntary changes that media people introduce through an awareness of the needs of the community they serve. That is why projects which throw light on media performance are to be welcomed.

The key to change will be the character of journalists. Over the years I have had the good fortune to meet many fine journalists who put their profession ahead of their advancement. I have met journalists, too, who have been vitally involved not only in reporting events but also in shaping them for the better, without compromising their journalistic integrity. These include a Dutch TV journalist who in the course of his interviewing met and won the trust of the German and Italian speaking leaders in the South Tyrol dispute and was able to bring them together and contribute to a settlement; a UPI bureau chief in the deep South of the United States who was able to defuse potential racial violence in a Southern college town; a young English journalist whose exposure of the medical dangers of working with asbestos led to changes in the law.

Let me tell you about a friend who died ten years ago. His name was Ahmet Emin Yalman, from Turkey, who was awarded the international Golden Pen of Freedom for his service to journalism. At the height of the bitter feelings between Greece and Turkey before Cyprus became independent, he, a Turkish editor, laid aside old prejudices, went to Athens and penned such conciliatory articles that the London *Times* wrote later that what he had written about Cyprus and Greek-Turkish relations helped create the atmosphere which made the independence agreements possible.

In 1952 Yalman was hit by a hail of bullets. His would-be assassin was a high school student, Hüseyin Üzmez, who was sentenced to 20 years imprisonment. Yalman kept in touch with Üzmez in prison, arranged for him to continue his legal studies there and even through his paper supported an amnesty which

would free him. At Yalman's death Üzmez wrote, "What a sad
coincidence that the very day I opened my lawyer's office in
Ankara, the radio announced his death. How many of us are able
to conquer even the hearts of our enemies as did Yalman."

The lives of Yalman and of those other journalists I mentioned
illustrate a principle which I discovered enshrined on the walls of
The Oregonian. It comes from the Oregon Code of Ethics of
Journalism. It reads: "It is not true that a newspaper should only
be as advanced in its ethical atmosphere as it conceives the average of its readers to be. No man who is not in ethical advance of
the average of his community should be in the profession of
journalism."

January 13, 1983

The cement of society

I HAVE A FRIEND who subscribes to the *Washington Post*. But she
never reads it the day it comes out. In that way she doesn't get too
worked up about dire predictions of imminent disaster. I also
know people who have discontinued their daily paper or don't
even watch television news, they just get too depressed. Indeed, a
lady who sat next to me on a plane this week said, "I haven't read
a paper for two months and I feel so much better, like when I gave
up smoking." Such an ostrich-like approach to the world is not
going to help much if disaster strikes, though I suppose it could
prevent a few ulcers in the meantime.

There is no doubt that there is a public disaffection with the
media and a growing distrust of journalism. And it's not just a
question of blaming the messenger. A survey last year showed
that the credibility of print and electronic journalists is at its
lowest point ever. Only 16% of those polled had "a great deal of
confidence" in the press as against 30% only ten years ago.

After Watergate and Vietnam investigative journalism was
king. But distressing incidents like the Janet Cooke fabrications
in the *Washington Post,* a completely fictional reportage on Cam-
bodia in the *New York Times* Magazine, and the latest supposed
revelations about Congressional homosexuality which proved

unfounded have helped undermine public faith in the press. In the last two years press defendants have lost 42 out of 47 libel cases which came before a jury.

This development, for which the journalistic profession must carry a large share of the responsibility, is a far greater threat to the freedom of the press in this country than any government or corporate or judicial attempts to get information suppressed. In fact, an article in *US News and World Report* last week says that many in the press fear that ultimately a hostile public may seek legal changes that would erode First Amendment guarantees of press freedom.

I have been thinking about these matters since I attended a Lake Oswego Chamber of Commerce lunch two weeks ago where representatives of local TV, radio and press were speaking. They said many good and helpful things but one or two comments worried me, particularly when they were discussing what was news. For instance, one well-known radio commentator said that if, for example, the Elks were to provide hundreds of eye glasses to people who needed them, it would not be news, they would only be doing their job. If an Elks treasurer absconded with the organization's money, that would be.

One prominent TV newsman, asked about whether the media weren't obsessed with negative or violent news, replied by parodying a desire for good news and describing how dull and insipid a newscast would be if it contained only news of the commonplace. Which, of course, nobody had asked for. What they were seeking was a better balance.

This particular TV man went on to say that there was nobody more self-critical than the TV journalist. That may be true but it is limited to in-house self-criticism. Let criticism come from outside the station and all self-criticism goes out the window. You're most likely to be told that you don't understand the business. That is one reason I welcome what the Assistant to the Publisher, Don Sterling, wrote in last week's *Oregonian*. He said that his paper favors the establishment of an Oregon Press Council. This would be an independent body that investigates complaints that the newsmedia have been inaccurate, unfair or unethical and then publishes its findings on the subject. "A news council," writes

Sterling, "can provide benefits for the newsmedia and the public alike by helping to bolster public confidence in the fairness, accuracy and integrity of their news sources."

Ultimately, of course, in our free society, the necessary changes will have to come from within—if they are not going to be imposed from without. This will not be achieved by press councils but by press peoples' consciences and their vision. They may need a new concept of their role in society, possibly even a new sense of what is news. A recent survey, referred to in the *Columbia Journalism Review,* shows that the profession is very divided on its definition anyway. There is little consensus on what makes news. Forty-one percent said that they gave priority to matters of consequence, 32% to subjects of interest "and most, Humpty Dumpty like, pronounced news to be whatever they said it was."

Some journalists define their role as basically an adversarial one, especially towards government. Certainly there are times when a newspaper may have to be ready to adopt such a stance whatever the risk entailed. But in the age in which we live one could perhaps legitimately question this assumption. One of the journalists at the lunch spoke of the growing intolerance of differences of opinion in the United States. Without doubt we are a fragmenting society with a multiplication of single-issue lobbies. Is the press perhaps meant to be the cement of society and the encourager of changes in lifestyle and attitude as well as the supplier of information needed to survive in our crumbling civilization?

The Oregon Code of Ethics of Journalism would be a reassurance to the disenchanted public and a considerable challenge to any journalist who took the time to read it. Its final point states: "We affirm the printed word, medium of global communication, is a means to the end of freeing the human mind from bigotry, hate and intolerance, and for the establishment of better living, international peace and justice to all."

October 7, 1982

3 Peace

Human nature

NEARLY SEVENTY YEARS AGO in the early stages of World War I British and German soldiers, as Christmas Day dawned, are supposed to have laid down their arms and cautiously entered no-man's-land to greet each other and talk a while before resuming their deadly business. No one gave the order to behave in this fashion, indeed neither High Command would have sanctioned such a fraternization if they had been asked to do so. It was somehow a spontaneous response to a deep longing in the human heart. For Christmas and thoughts of peace go naturally together.

It is extraordinary when so many people long for peace that it should prove so elusive. With the burgeoning of peace movements, with the widespread fears that the proliferation of nuclear weapons may lead us willy-nilly into a war that could destroy the world, it is important to be all the time trying to get perspective on the subject. Since I became involved in a peace commission last year I have been asking myself some questions about our work for peace. Is it inclusive enough, is it broad enough, is it fundamental enough and is there a challenge in it to the way each of us lives?

My uncle is a pacifist. Rather than serve in the armed forces he worked in World War I with refugees and in World War II with radium. My father volunteered before he was conscripted in both wars, fighting in the trenches and serving on the general staff. I never had the sense that one was less peace-loving than the other, that one was more selfless or indeed more Christian. Both made great sacrifices for their country and for their beliefs.

To me any peace effort worthy of the name and standing a chance of reaching its objective has to be one that can enlist the sympathy and energy and sacrifice of both sorts of men. Too many so-called peace workers seem to be so rigid in their approach, so self-righteous in their condemnation of others that they end up making their own fellow countrymen and women, even their own duly elected representatives, their enemies.

I wonder, too, whether we may not need that more inclusive approach to nations as well as individuals. Peace is after all not just the absence of war and we should perhaps be looking for those activities where cooperation would be more profitable than confrontation. Neither the Soviet Union nor the Western governments, with honorable exceptions, have shown much enthusiasm about tackling the world's great economic disparities. It has been calculated that the amount of money spent every two weeks by the governments of the world on armaments would enable us to feed, water, house, educate and give healthcare to every individual in the world. Is it too much to hope that it is in this field that the great power rivalry may one day be channelled?

It is just possible that the future of the world is threatened less by a nuclear holocaust than by the terrible and growing gap between rich and poor nations for which our arms race is partly responsible. As the Brandt Commission concluded, "More arms are not making the world safer, only poorer."

Vital as it is for all of us to work towards nuclear disarmament, our present preoccupation with the subject could blind us to one awkward fact. If every nuclear weapon were suddenly miraculously removed from the earth it is doubtful if we would be any nearer peace. The situation could be even more dangerous for misguided politicians or dictators might be more prepared to initiate a war with conventional weapons than with nuclear ones. A more fundamental approach is called for.

The truth is that the rock on which peacemaking efforts founder is human nature, the unresolved hurts, the frustrated ambitions, the desire for revenge. And we need to be tackling these with the same determination we apply to opposing nuclear weaponry. The reason that we don't, of course, is that it is a tougher job and that it means that we need to be sure that these elements are absent from our own lives. When Christ said, "Blessed are the peacemakers for they shall be called the children of God," I form the impression that he was talking not about those who only demonstrated for peace but those who also lived a quality of peace in their own lives.

Perhaps this Christmas we could each consider whether there is anyone we feel divided from and make tomorrow, the birthday of the Prince of Peace, the day when we put the matter right. We would be true peacemakers.

December 24, 1981

Forgiveness

MANY PEOPLE were surprised and indeed heartened to see the *Time* magazine cover story in early January "A pardon from the Pontiff—a lesson in forgiveness for a troubled world." Summing up the significance of the remarkable meeting between Pope John Paul II and his would-be killer, Turkish gunman Mehmet Ali Agca, Lance Morrow wrote, "Forgiveness is not an impulse that is much in favor. It is a mysterious and sublime idea in many ways. The prevalent style in the world runs more to the high-plains drifter, to the hard, cold eye of the avenger, to a numb remorselessness. Forgiveness does not look much like a tool for survival in a bad world. But that is what it is."

I began to think of instances where forgiveness played a role not only between individuals but was encouraged at government level. For instance, in a number of African countries.

The night the Nigerian Civil War ended, the Head of State, Major General Yakubu Gowon, put forward reconciliation as the basis of his policy. At the height of that war he had reminded his fellow countrymen and women on both sides of the example of reconciliation between France and Germany. "We cannot, however, achieve national reconciliation," he said, "by quoting the experience of other peoples. Honestly, I believe it is part of the African character to forgive and try to forget. Unless we try to forget, it will be more difficult to truly forgive." Nigeria has other pressing problems now but that policy of reconciliation prevailed to such an extent that it removed much of the bitter legacy of the war, a fact confirmed to me by senior people on both sides. No victors, no vanquished, became the official line.

When Jomo Kenyatta, as Prime Minister of Kenya, first met the white settlers who had fought against him in the independence struggle, he told them, "I have made many mistakes; please forgive me. You have made mistakes; I forgive you.' I want you to stay and farm and farm well in this country. Let us join hands and work for the benefit of Kenya and not for the benefit of one particular community. This is what I beg you to believe. This is the policy of our Government." There is no doubt that this approach was key to the development of that country. Without it AP would never have been able to send out a story on Kenya, as they did last month, which was headlined in *The Oregonian,* "A multiracial model in black Africa."

And when Zimbabwe's new Prime Minister, Robert Mugabe, first spoke to his people after a bloody seven-year war of independence, he, too, said, "Let us beat our swords into ploughshares. Forgive others and forget. Join hands in a new amity together. Let us constitute a oneness derived from our common objectives and total commitment to build a great Zimbabwe that will be the pride of all Africa." Now the survival, the word *Time* used, of Zimbabwe may depend on how far that noble aim can transcend the other pressures internally and externally on that country.

For the Kenyans, the Nigerians, the Zimbabweans, of all races, after years of repression, cruelty, torture, humiliation and personal loss, the act of forgiveness was no small thing as it was not for the French and Germans who fought three wars in seventy years and whose example was quoted by General Gowon.

One lady who was pivotal in that Franco-German reconciliation is Irene Laure from France who was in Portland some time back. She was a leader of the resistance movement in World War II, her son was tortured by the Gestapo. All the same, soon after the war, she reached out her hand to the Germans. She says, "Can you think what it meant for me to go there? In my heart I had willed the ruins of World War II. I am a mother and grandmother. I am a Socialist and all my life I have talked about fraternity, yet I had longed for a whole people to be destroyed. I had to ask forgiveness for my hatred from those people who were living in the ruins. I had to ask forgiveness from 50,000 women whom I saw, grey with fatigue, clearing the rubble in Berlin. I do not forget the ruins in my own, or other countries, that the Germans caused. Not at all. But the thing I had to do was to face my own hatred and the part it played in dividing Europe, and to ask forgiveness for it."

We admire, at a distance, such people. We almost take for granted what they do. We expect as a matter of course that black and white in Africa should be able to live together after all they have been through. I sometimes wonder whether we are prepared, often in less traumatic circumstances, to reach out a forgiving hand to those we differ from politically or ideologically.

Those of us, like the Pope, who call ourselves Christian, may have to set the fashion in this regard. It is worth reflecting on the perspective of Mikhail Borodin, the Chicago teacher who had a key part in trying to establish Communism in China. "The Christian doctrine of forgiveness, so often preached, so little practised and seemingly so innocuous," he said, "is the greatest stumbling block in the path of Communism."

January 26, 1984

I am for war!

"I AM FOR WAR." If I went round saying that, people would think I was off my rocker. "I am for peace." Ah, that's a different matter. Or is it? To be blunt, I find the second remark only a degree more meaningful than the first. To say you are for peace is, in my view, almost irrelevant to the process of peacemaking. It may salve your conscience, it may increase your acceptance by some of your peers. It may give you the illusion that you are doing something. It may make you feel better than those who don't go round saying they are for peace. But I find it offensive to divide the country into those who are for peace and those who are not. As Dan Rather of CBS had to point out in Portland last week, and this was a factual statement not an endorsement, President Reagan is for a stronger military precisely because he thinks it will ensure peace.

Some people seem fascinated by false alternatives, chase after instant solutions, generously apportion all the blame to others. It can be a counter-productive approach.

Helen Caldicott, founder of Physicians for Social Responsibility, made a powerful emotional appeal at a meeting of the City Club and the World Affairs Council earlier this month. Her basic message was, "Get rid of Reagan." It fell on receptive ears. This Australian doctor who believes that she needs to move audiences to tears managed to almost equate Reagan with Hitler, label the Congress as stupid and pathetic, Weinberger and Shultz as weak, the Soviet leadership as geriatric, even disown Margaret Thatcher as a woman and call all women wimps while at the same time extolling the virtues of love and the message of Christ, particularly the need to see the beam in your own eye rather than the mote in the other person's. "We've got six months to save the earth," she said dramatically.

This dedicated, sincere, passionate advocate is entitled to her views. She can be admired for the way she marshals her arguments. That's what the American way of life is all about — the freedom for all, including an Australian and an Englishman, to say what they think. And to differ.

When I opened my mail the other day I found a five-page letter from the Honorable James G. Watt. I don't know how many thousands of others got it too. It was addressed to "Dear fellow American" which I am definitely not. He enclosed a letter from President Reagan who tells me, "Your work is well known to me," which is patently nonsense. Watt's appeal was not unlike Caldicott's except that his primary purpose was to get some money from me. She says, six months to save the earth. He says, "If President Reagan fails in his programs our future is lost." If Reagan loses, he underlines the point, "America as you want it to be will be lost forever."

He, too, is entitled to his views. When it comes to November the public can make their choice. That is their right. As Rather also said, responding to a question on the peace issue, "Let us not kid ourselves, if we do not like nuclear policy, we have the capacity to change it."

But I have a feeling that whatever the election result, whether you regard Reagan as the problem or Reagan as the answer, the basic issues will remain much the same. Life is not so simple that a change of presidents will solve all our problems on the home front, in Latin America or in US-Soviet relations. I know that may not be the perspective of the man who greeted me when I arrived at the KBOO studio last week, the morning after the unexpected defeat of Mayor Ivancie. He met me with the enthusiastic comment, "It gives you hope about Reagan, doesn't it."

I found that the recent Lewis and Clark College conference on Central America was a good corrective to simplistic analysis. Not only did we have there the Ambassadors of El Salvador and Nicaragua, a State Department spokesman and the former mayor of San Salvador now in exile who all painted their picture of the situation. But we also had distinguished academics who refused to tailor the facts to fit a particular political perspective. Their views were not, of course, entirely welcomed by those who see a Commie behind every cactus and those who wouldn't see red in any circumstances.

I happened to switch on Cable Television's C-Span and caught some of the debate in the House of Representatives on Central America. I'm sorry to have to inform Helen Caldicott that there was nothing stupid or pathetic about it. It was sincere, serious men and women grappling with very complex issues where there is no easy option and no safe consequences for this nation which, whether it likes it or not, has thrust upon it the mantle of world leadership.

I also listened to the House debate on the MX and defense policy. Again there were strong, well argued, thoughtful contributions from all sides. Some highly contradictory. I was impressed by the words of two Congressmen in particular who were each responding to House colleagues with directly opposed views. I felt their approach is one that we could all beneficially adopt. Congressman Herbert Bateman said, "Nothing from my mouth impugns the honesty of my opponent." Congressman Ronald Dellums said, "You and I are equal in our passion for our country and our passion for peace."

May 24, 1984

Neutrality

I ONCE STAYED with a family in Europe and, happening by chance
to put my hand under my bed, encountered something metal. On
closer examination it turned out, to my shock, to be a weapon
which to a layman like me looked suspiciously like a machine
gun. I wonder if you can guess what country I was in. It wasn't
Ireland. It wasn't Italy. It was peace-loving Switzerland.

A lot is said about Swiss neutrality and jokes are made at
Switzerland's expense. I remember in the film *The Third Man*
Orson Welles, I think it was, saying to a Swiss, "One hundred and
fifty years of peace and what have you produced — the cuckoo
clock!" But what many people, apart from potential aggressors,
don't realize is that Switzerland's peace and security stem not
from wishy-washyness or a pacifist approach to life but from a
tough defense policy that takes full advantage of the country's
geographical features.

There's a certain ruggedness and realism about the world on
the part of the Swiss. Though I will admit I was surprised when a
senior Swiss ambassador, talking about issues like the nuclear
freeze, said that paradoxically the peace movements were a great
danger to world balance and to peace. He told me, only half
jokingly, that he thought that the Nobel Peace Prize should be
given jointly to NATO and the Warsaw Pact. Their balance of
forces had prevented war over the last thirty years. He quoted the
Swiss foreign minister as saying recently that future historians
would be hard put to explain today's European generation who
were more afraid of weapons that were there to defend them than
those which threatened them. The ambassador saw this as a kind
of Western spiritual decadence which, he said, was shocking and
dangerous because it was a source of false calculations on the part
of the East. "There are higher values in life than peace," he said.
"One is freedom."

Freedom is something the Swiss certainly feel strongly about.
They are proud of their democracy. Anyone must be aware of that
who has been in Switzerland on National Day or who has visited
the *Rütli*, the historic spot where in 1291 three cantons joined to

form the base of today's Swiss Confederation. And a big factor in Swiss pride is the nature of citizen involvement in national defense.

Which brings me to that experience in the Swiss home. Every man in Switzerland does army service and every man keeps his automatic rifle, 50 rounds of ammunition, uniform and equipment at home. Only the physically or mentally handicapped are excused service, and, for limited periods, people in certain occupations like policemen or firemen. There are no exemptions on religious or moral grounds. Conscientious objectors, of which there are few, are tried by military courts and usually sent to prison. The standing forces at any one moment number only 3000 excluding the 30,000 recruits who start seventeen weeks basic training each year. But, and it is a very big but, in 48 hours Switzerland can mobilize 640,000 men, a tenth of its population —the highest concentration of military manpower in Europe.

The permanent military establishment consists of about 800 officers and the same number of non-commissioned officers. The rest of the population are eligible for military service for 30 to 35 years which in practice amounts to a number of weeks each year. Most Swiss men are also involved in many voluntary service-related activities. Those aged 20 to 32 constitute the main combat force of 300,000. The territorial force of 200,000 is drawn from those aged 33 to 40 and the veteran reserve of 140,000 is made up of those from 43 to 55. Women have only a minor role in the military as volunteers in non-combat jobs in a women's auxiliary corps. Of course, in the event of a general mobilization their civilian role would be particularly important.

The aim of Swiss defense, according to Dr. H. R. Kurz of the Swiss Federal Military Department, is to appear to a would-be aggressor so strong and effective that he would desist because he would realize the unreasonably high cost of an attack. An aggressor must be made aware, he says, that Switzerland will never allow herself to be blackmailed, nor will she surrender without a struggle. It was Switzerland's announced and obvious readiness to fight at the start of World War II that made Hitler hesitate to attack the country. It is interesting that at that dangerous time the Swiss Commander, General Henri Guisan, gathered together all the officer corps at that historic *Rütli* plateau where they made a solemn pledge to defend their country.

As a consequence of Swiss neutrality her army exists solely for defense and is totally self-sufficient. Switzerland possesses no nuclear weapons and has no plans to acquire any in the foreseeable future. Despite her neutrality, however, Switzerland's present defense strategy is based on the belief that any attack by conventional forces would come from the Soviet bloc and would lead to general war with the Western nuclear powers on Switzerland's side.

Switzerland is speeding up its civil defense with an already far-advanced program aimed at supplying every member of the population with a fully protected anti-nuclear shelter by the year 2000. If some doomsters' predictions about nuclear war are fulfilled, it sounds as if the Swiss might inherit the earth. Not, however, because they are meek.

December 12, 1982

Nuclear freeze

THE OREGONIAN wrote recently, "Opposition to the nuclear freeze movement can be viewed only as support for a policy of fighting and winning a nuclear war."

What nonsense.

I know plenty of people who oppose the freeze and who do not support such a policy. Indeed, they oppose the freeze because they feel that it may bring war closer not prevent it.

It is this kind of *us* and *them* thinking which turns off a lot of people.

I honestly am not sure what to think about the freeze. I have read reams of material for and against. I can see one real advantage in its adoption. It would be a dramatic psychological gesture that could conceivably help halt the seemingly endless spiral of more and more nuclear weapons and thereby release money for more urgent social needs at home and abroad. That alone would be a tremendous achievement. And it is hard at the moment to see any other initiative which could come near such a result. It might also reduce the element of fear which is poisoning our children's lives, which is used shamelessly by both sides, and which is a poor basis for rational decision about the future.

But it would be hard to see that a freeze would achieve more than that. I don't think that it would much reduce the threat posed by the use either intentionally or accidentally of nuclear weapons. The arms would still exist. 50,000 nuclear warheads possessed by the two great powers are not going to go away. It is estimated that the eight nations now having nuclear weapons will have been joined by 27 more in the next eight years.

Some opponents of the freeze say that it would lock the US into a position of inferiority strategically vis-a-vis the Soviet Union. Those for or against the freeze parade lists of weapons and warheads and delivery systems which sustain or disprove this particular attitude. It reminds me of what an Australian political figure told me in Portland last year. Much of politics, he said, consists of bolstering the arguments that support your view and suppressing any facts that contradict it. The trouble, he went on, is that if you do that for too long you end up by actually believing your own propaganda. "Statistically," says an article in *The Christian Science Monitor* last week, "the question is whether a freeze would ensure balance or institutionalize Soviet supremacy and that depends on whose count you take."

President Reagan ruffled a few feathers last week when he suggested that the Soviets were behind the freeze movement. As the Soviet intention in this field is well documented the rush to deny any influence seems to some critics to reveal a certain naiveté on the part of some in the freeze movement.

Some open-minded people would have more sympathy with the freeze if its proponents would admit that the United States might be in a position of inferiority but that it is a calculated risk which is worth taking, that there might be some Soviet inspiration in the peace movement but it is far outweighed by the rightness of the cause. If they would also concede that nuclear weapons had helped keep the peace for over thirty years and that there was an element of risk in departing from a tried and proven ingredient of our security arrangements.

Some people with a feel for history are worried about the pacifist and unilateralist wing of the peace movement. In their concern about what the whole movement might be saying about America to any would-be aggressor, they overlook the fact that the wording of the freeze initiative calls for it to be mutual and verifiable. They cite the 1930's when a peace movement in Britain fed in Hitler the idea that when the chips were down Britons would not fight and thereby contributed to the onset of World War II. I was interested at the beginning of the Falklands crisis that a Russian said to me, "You have to fight. Otherwise the Soviets will believe that in the final analysis the West will do nothing but talk." For, after all, the credibility of the nation's defense hangs on that question, "Will they fight?"

My own personal concern in this whole area is something different. I would like to see the freeze debate broadened out so that we start to wage total peace and are not just preoccupied with nuclear weapons. For wars have never been caused by weapons — though occasionally by lack of them. They have been caused by individuals' hatred and greed, by national grievances and historic injustices, and sometimes by misunderstandings. That is where the action should also be.

That is a more challenging assignment than standing up to Washington or demonstrating against somebody else, because it requires us to eliminate from our own lives any prejudices or resentments we may have against individuals or countries as a first step in peacemaking. It is an assignment which could draw the best out of all of us — pacifist or professional soldier or somewhere in between. It could unite the country and perhaps lead us to find ways of removing the mistrust between continents. It is a commitment for life and not just for a legislative victory.

It is important to recognize that even if the freeze were entirely successful, the fundamental work of creating the conditions for peace would have only just begun.

November 18, 1982

Living peace

IT MUST HAVE OCCURRED to you sometimes that "peaceful" is not the adjective one first associates with some people in the peace movement. One sees too often fearful, angry people trying to convince others of the urgency of their protest. The peacemakers at times show more of the demons they are fighting than of the peace they want to bring.

This is a phenomenon which I have observed and which was underlined in a conversation with a fascinating Catholic priest, Father Henry Nouwen, recently appointed Professor in the Harvard Divinity School with whom I spent a morning on a recent trip to Boston.

I had first heard of Father Nouwen last year when friends began to write me quoting from him or recommending his books as ones with particularly profound spiritual insight which had helped them in their daily lives. Some of his more recent books include *Clowning in Rome, The Way of the Heart, Making All Things New, Compassion* and *A Letter of Consolation.* For ten years he taught at Yale and part of each year he is in South America.

Father Nouwen told me of his concern that people get so involved in Christian issues, women's issues, third world issues, nuclear issues, that they do not nurture deeply enough what he calls the personal relationship with Christ which alone can make a creative relationship with these issues possible.

Coming from his background and training it is perhaps natural that he should be addressing his remarks to Christians and thinking in Christian terms. Though he is the first to reject what he described to me as "mountaintop spirituality." The Dutch-born priest is deeply involved in today's issues and on today's wavelength. He had just put up a notice for a retreat he was conducting and found within an hour that it was oversubscribed with 75 students. I thought that a paragraph I came across in an article he had written some years ago illustrated his "common touch." It was in the magazine *America,* entitled "Unceasing Prayer," and was about the need for discipline in our thought life. "During the most solemn moments," he wrote, "we may find ourselves thinking the most banal thoughts. While listening to a sermon about God's love, we find ourselves wondering about the haircut of the preacher. While reading a spiritual book, we suddenly realize that our mind is busy with the question of how much peanut butter and how much jam to put on our next sandwich. While watching a beautiful ceremony at St. Peters, we notice ourselves trying to figure out where in the Vatican the laundromat is located in which those thousands of surplices will be cleaned after the service."

Actually, this article about "Unceasing Prayer" is very much at the heart, it seemed to me, of his current thinking about peacemaking. He wants to develop a spirituality of peacemaking, and indeed kindly loaned me a draft of a book he is writing on the subject. Christians, he believes, do not have an obligation to give some attention to war prevention or some of their free time. What we are called to, he says, is a life of peacemaking in which all we do, say, think or dream is part of our concern to bring peace in the world.

He has obviously not found it easy to come out openly in a commitment to "peace." He was brought up in a milieu where peace movements, anti-nuclear activists and the like were seen as expressions of immaturity or even of Russian-inspired anti-patriotism. He has been an army chaplain. He is still skeptical of the value of many anti-war activities and put off by the conflicts and divisions between peacemakers and nervous about being in the company of people whose lifestyle, ideology and tactics contradict the essence of the peace Christ spoke about.

Nevertheless he believes that it must become the priority of Christians to save humanity from collective suicide. Although the Beatitudes, he says, are for all time, at different ages in history different ones have been given more emphasis than others. And this century was clearly the century of the peacemaker.

But to be a peacemaker today required a life of prayer if one was not going to be caught in the world's panic, fear and anxiety. "The same fear that leads warmakers to war starts to effect the peacemaker," he writes. "Then the words of anger and hostility that create divisions and conflicts also enter into the language of the peacemakers. Then the sense of urgency and emergency that motivates the rapid escalation of the arms race also becomes the driving force of the peacemakers. Then indeed the strategy of war and the strategy of peace have become the same and peacemaking has lost its heart."

He does not feel that after reading his *Spirituality of Peacemaking* a person necessarily has to do or say anything different than before. But everyone should come to realize that nothing he is doing or saying is worth doing if it does not lead to peace. "Peacemaking is a way of living that involves our whole being all the time."

There is not time to go into the ramifications that follow a life of unceasing prayer or explain what he means when he says that prayer as living in the presence of God is not a spiritual fallout shelter but is the most radical peace action we can imagine. Or to outline the stages he recommends following so that a radical "no" to death in all its forms can mean the beginning of a spiritual home that no Cruise missile or Trident submarine can destroy. One hopes that his book will be published soon and read by many.

Father Nouwen in a way envisions an order of peacemakers all over the world, monks of the nuclear age, men and women, married and single, walking alone, walking together, occasionally visible, more often contemplative, a network of resistance to evil and the powers of death, a community of hope held together by a rule of faith, their main concern to do the will of God, not their own.

If Mahatma Gandhi could oversimplify his work by saying, "My life is my message," then perhaps Father Nouwen's challenge to us is to be able to say, "Peace is my life."

April 28, 1983

Oregon teaparty

RECENTLY I attended what I thought was going to be a quiet tea party in Lake Oswego. It turned out differently.

It showed me that exchanges alone do not in themselves promote peace and also illuminated for me a vital and often overlooked ingredient of peacemaking.

A good friend, concerned about how to improve relations between the United States and the Soviet Union, had invited a
Russian couple to meet a well-known Oregonian peace activist
just returned from the Soviet Union and to see his color slides of
Moscow.

As I had staying with me a Norwegian colleague who had
written about Soviet dissidents, we were invited too.

We came to listen. We did not know whether the Russians were
exiles or planned to return home, though that soon became clear.

As the display of slides clicked on, accompanied by the enthusiastic commentary of the peace activist, who was excited by
the possibilities of communicating on the cultural level, the Russian couple stirred uneasily. Obviously they had some idea in
advance of what to expect, for eventually they produced a book in
Russian, *Notes of a Dissident,* by Andrei Amalrik.

The wife proceeded to read from the book, translating as she
went: "We have no right to condemn people because their own
problems disturb them more than all our sufferings. The more so,
we have no right to demand that they enter into our skins and feel
how hard pressed we are. But we do have the right to tell them: if
you value not only freedom for yourself but also the principle of
freedom, think well before entering into an intellectual dialogue
with the country where the very idea of freedom is perverted."

I suppose if at that point in our conversation we had shown
more understanding of what the Russians had lived through, the
encounter might have been more immediately fruitful. The peace
activist, because he was so well-meaning and ready to believe the
best, I guess, found it hard to accept the Russian couples' suspi-
cion that the KGB might take advantage of his overtures.

There has been, as most newspaper readers will have noticed, a
recent visit to Portland of a group of Soviet citizens. I do not refer
to the officials attending the Lewis and Clark College conference
but to the supposedly unofficial group. The peace activist saw
such exchanges as an advance. You needed to begin people-to-
people, he said, and not raise controversial issues (like
Sakharov). The Russian couple revealed, however, that at the
same time the Soviet delegation were all smiles publicly, one of
the group had taken them aside, out of sight of the KGB super-

visor, and talking in Russian, had told them that the persecution in the Soviet Union was getting worse.

The harder the Russian couple at the tea tried to get across their perspective, the less their concerns seemed to get through. The two sides, as they turned out to be, were talking past each other. The Russian husband finally walked out into the kitchen and told our host, "I don't trust that man." Then the couple left, without shaking hands.

My Norwegian friend and I naturally talked quite a bit about the tea. He had been condemned to death by the Nazis for his role in the resistance movement. He understood what the Russian couple felt. What would he have thought about someone who visited Nazi Germany before World War II on a people-to-people basis and, if the concentration camps had been known about, refused to raise the issue with their hosts. Peace without freedom, he told me, means little to those who have once lost freedom.

He quoted Alexander Solzhenitsyn: "In our crowded world you have to pay a tax for freedom. You cannot love freedom for yourself alone and quietly agree to a situation where the majority of humanity, spread over the greater part of the globe, is subjected to violence and oppression. Freedom is indivisible and one has to take a moral attitude toward it."

To make peace our sole aim is to open ourselves up to blackmail and to surrender the field to those for whom peace is a tactic. To make freedom the only issue is to deny the dangers of war that many freedom-loving people sense. Peace is too big an issue to be left only to the peaceworkers, freedom is too vital to be left only to those who have lost it.

Peace and freedom call for the visionary quality of my peaceworker friend who is not cynical, though he may be naive, and the reality of the Russian couple who may be bitter but are not fuzzy. A synthesis of the two, through an end to naiveté and to bitterness, would be irresistible.

I'm looking forward to the next tea party.

February 16, 1984

4 Movies

Chariots of Fire

I WOULD LIKE to talk today about a movie. Not because it needs any recommendation from me — several of my friends who have gone to see it recently have not been able to get in, such is its popularity. Not because it is a British film of which I can be justly proud. But because it is a really great film that speaks on a profound level to all who see it.

I am talking of *Chariots of Fire,* a true story of two British runners who won gold medals in the 1924 Olympics — Eric Liddell, a Scot who ran for his faith and later served as a Christian missionary in China and actually died there in prison in World War II, and Harold Abraham, a Jew who ran for his people and, until his death a few years ago, was the distinguished dean of British athletics. The purpose of the film, however, is not to portray Christianity versus Judaism but rather to portray the supremacy of ethics and conscience over expediency. "There is an ethical core inside everyone which is longing to be addressed," says the film's producer, David Puttnam. "*Chariots of Fire* addresses it, which is why it is successful."

There have been many excellent reviews in the press here so I won't go in detail into the qualities of the film, the casting and production, the music, etc., but, instead, talk about the motivation of this man who made it, which is the key to its quality.

David Puttnam is known to Americans as the producer of *Midnight Express.* He made it essentially to prove that British film makers could beat the Americans at their own game and produce a film that would be a technical success around the world. But, he says, if you aim for a success, that is what you get and nothing more. Puttnam was appalled at the reactions to the film. For instance, at the Cannes Film Festival, during a particularly violent sequence the audience leapt onto their seats and urged on the protagonists. He became determined to prove that he had an ethical self as well as a technical one.

As a young man he had seen *A Man for All Seasons,* the classic film where Sir Thomas More, played by Paul Schofield, goes to his death rather than compromise his principles. Puttnam had come out of the cinema profoundly moved and changed by the experience. He began to look for a modern parallel, a story in which for ethical reasons the hero did something which was, in worldly terms, madness, and after which the audience would leave the cinema convinced that the hero had been right in his action and that under certain circumstances they would have done the same.

Such is *Chariots of Fire*. In contemporary terms it is madness that the devout Christian, Liddell, should refuse to run in an Olympic heat simply because it is scheduled for a Sunday, but the audience is behind him in his decision.

The most important scene in the film, according to Puttnam, is where all the power of the British Establishment is mobilized, including the Prince of Wales and the Chairman of the British Olympic Committee, to try to persuade Liddell to act against his conscience. "That is every day for each of us," says Puttnam. "The board room, the office, the local committee meeting, where we make our petty compromises with truth and principle."

I personally find another moment in that same scene to be very stirring. It is when Lord Lindsay, the young, aristocratic friend of Liddell, offers to withdraw from a heat for which he has qualified and which has been scheduled for a week day, thus sacrificing his own chance of the medal so that Liddell can run.

Another person who stands out in a way in the film is Aubrey Montague, a young runner in the Olympic team who didn't win any medal. Puttnam calls him the real hero of the film. He says he is each of us, the ordinary man who does not succeed, the one who doesn't win but who makes the world go round.

Puttnam points out the difference between Abraham's and Liddell's reactions to success. For Abraham there was total emptiness and anti-climax after attaining his goal. That, says Puttnam, was his experience after *Midnight Express*. Liddell ran for God. He enjoyed success and he shared it. In one of the last scenes when the returning heroes are welcomed back from France by a cheering crowd, Liddell holds up Aubrey Montague's hand to them for acclaim.

Puttnam is an honest man. "In some ways, Harold Abraham is the man I am," he says. "Eric Liddell is the man I would like to be." "I fear success," he told some of my friends in London the other day. "I know so many people who have been ruined by it and none who have been improved by it. I have learned how to handle failure but I am terrified of success. If one remains always successful then one has not been stretched enough. I hope that I will one day make a film that really is wonderful and it will fail because it will be ahead of its time."

March 25, 1982

Gandhi

I WENT TO THE MOVIES last weekend during the Super Bowl and met hundreds of Americans doing likewise. What had torn them away from their TV sets but that marvellous film *Gandhi*. We sat enthralled by the story of a man whose character, dedication and shrewdness routed an imperial power and is still a challenge to a world torn with hatred and division.

To say that the National Board of Review and the New York Film Critics Circle both voted *Gandhi* the best film of 1982 and that it won five Golden Globe awards hardly does it justice. Many films have won awards but few have had as much to say about life, past, present and possibly future.

For those who have grown up since Indian independence in 1947 it will be an introduction to one of the greatest figures of the twentieth century. For older ones it will be a reminder of his monumental achievement in seizing the imagination of hundreds of millions of Indians of different backgrounds and mobilizing them in the struggle for freedom. On another level it must surely repay India many times over for the investment put into the film by the Indian National Film Development Corporation. More than thirty books on Gandhi have been published for the first time or reissued in the last few months.

Ralph Nader, the consumer advocate, told *The New York Times* that he had gained from the film a new appreciation of the technique that Gandhi used to mobilize the Indian people behind the independence movement, particularly how he had transformed the consumer issues of salt and cloth into the larger struggle for independence. But to see the film as a lesson in how to organize for a political object, as Nader does, is to see it on a superficial level. Indeed, Ben Kingsley, the Royal Shakespeare Company actor who has so convincingly found his way to the inner Gandhi in his portrayal of the title role, says, "I don't think Gandhi thought in terms of winning. If Gandhi, or me as Gandhi, makes the other person feel a better human being then the victory is to more decent people in the room."

It is not just a message either about non-violence; though Coretta King, who attended the Indian premiere in Delhi, was deeply touched and referred to Gandhi as "the man whose philosophy probably was the single most influential element in shaping my husband's belief in non-violence."

The film seemed to me to be about purity of motive. At one point in the film Gandhi even states that he does not want independence if it is achieved by violence. "I want to change their minds," he says about the British, "not kill them for weaknesses we all possess." He asks one of his colleagues, "Do you fight to change things or do you fight to punish?" It is a film about militant goodness. At one point someone refers to passive resistance. "I have never been passive about anything," he responds.

As the film opens one notices that it is dedicated to Jawaharlal Nehru, Earl Mountbatten and Motilal Kothari. And who might Kothari be?

Twenty years ago British film director Richard Attenborough went one evening to an art auction to raise funds for the Save the Children Fund. He bought a bust of Pandit Nehru by Epstein. The next morning early he had a 'phone call. "My name is Motilal Kothari. I have to see you," said the caller. At lunch a few days later he told the Englishman that he must make a film about Gandhi and gave him Louis Fischer's biography. Attenborough took the book on vacation and could not put it down. He came to that incident which appears in the film where Gandhi is pushed off a pavement in South Africa for being non-white. Attenborough read Gandhi's comment that he was amazed that men should feel themselves honored by the humiliation of their fellow human beings. "I felt I couldn't wait any longer," he says. "I went to the telephone. I remember it was a public telephone in a passage in a little *pension* where we were staying. And I yelled down the 'phone, 'Mr. Kothari, I will give up anything and everything to be able to make this movie.' " That was in 1962.

Attenborough kept his word. "I had to sell the cars," he says, "and mortgage the house and hock my paintings. I've given up forty acting roles and a dozen director's assignments." He told Gandhi's grandson, Rajmohan, three years ago, "My 23-year-old daughter can't remember a time when Daddy wasn't going to make Gandhi. She has to wonder what else Daddy does with his life." At that time there was a criticism that a foreign director should make such a film and Rajmohan Gandhi wrote, "Attenborough reveals the passion of a distinguished film-maker to share with the world an experience and understanding of Gandhi that has touched him and I find the passion worthy of support."

Though regarding himself as a cynic and finding much of today's visual arts, cinema and television deprecatory and cynical, Attenborough believes that Gandhi more than anyone else in the last decades has been an example of how people can live in a civilized manner. "If we don't in the cinema make the cry for compassion, and the plea for tolerance and understanding," he says, "then we deny the very genuius of the medium which it is for us a privilege to work in."

A critic in *The Oregonian* has suggested that perhaps the better you knew Gandhi, the less you liked the film. This is hardly borne out by the reviews in the Indian press and the response of his family and those who worked with him. The film critic in the *Hindustan Times,* for instance, wrote, "Skeptics have been proved wrong. Attenborough's is a wholly satisfying work. Gandhi steps forward from these vivid frames with all the force of legend and all the human detail and frailty of a real person." The critic in the country's largest paper, *Indian Express,* commented, "It has in it the possibility of restoring Gandhi to India."

I had a letter this week from one who was on that 1930 march to the sea to make salt which is so well dramatized in the film. He is 82-year-old Haridas Mazumdar. "I had tears in my eyes three or four times," he says. "The film is a profoundly moving experience and historically very accurate. You sit through three and a half hours spell-bound, bewitched as though you had been in your seat only fifteen minutes. It is an authentic portrayal of Gandhi's development and character."

It is humbling for an Englishman to see the terrible Amritsar massacre and for a Christian to see the way Gandhi is rejected by churchmen in South Africa. Yet one is heartened by the example of Charlie, the Christian minister who became one of Gandhi's closest friends and then was ready to withdraw from his side so as not to compromise the freedom struggle. This is C. F. Andrews whom Gandhi used to call, after his initials, Christ's faithful apostle. One is struck also by the dedication of Miraben Slade, who has only recently died, the daughter of a British admiral who forsook everything to come and serve in Gandhi's *ashram*.

The most moving moment in the film for me is when Gandhi is fasting to get the Hindu-Muslim killings stopped. A Hindu thug is reluctant to surrender his sword. He tells Gandhi that he is already living in hell because he has killed a Muslim baby, bashing it to death against a wall. "I know a way out of hell," says Gandhi. And proceeds to tell the anguished man to adopt a child whose parents have been killed. "And make sure he is a Muslim," he says, pausing to allow the thought to sink in before adding, "and raise him as one."

In an early scene Charlie tells a church congregation in South Africa, "What Mr. Gandhi has forced us to do is to ask questions about ourselves."

Through the film Gandhi continues to do so.

February 3, 1983

5 American life

Hunger

AT THE AGE OF 21 I was sitting in a dining car in an Indian train when we rolled into a station. Outside the window emaciated people, including small children, watched as I finished my meal, all the time appealing with gestures for something to eat. That experience helped confirm in me a commitment to live in a way to help answer injustice.

Nowadays the plight of people in less developed countries is regularly brought to our attention through television, often evoking a generous response. But sometimes we are so cushioned by a comfort that we have grown used to and don't notice that we can be quite oblivious to needs in our very midst.

I was not aware—I don't know if you are aware—that March has been named by Governor Atiyeh "Hunger Awareness Month." As he says, "Hunger is not a stranger to many of our citizens, and many of hunger's victims are not strangers — they are our neighbors." He urges us to share resources, to support and work with food distribution programs, and to develop a greater awareness of the needs of others so that hunger can be eliminated.

All sorts of Commissions, Presidential and otherwise, have been looking into hunger at home and overseas. All sorts of people have been making statements, some sensitive, some less so. All sorts of instant judgments are bandied about, from the allegation that all our aid gets skimmed off into Swiss bank accounts to the suggestion that people join bread lines because they like to. It has almost become fashionable in some Western circles, even religious ones, to maintain that the poverty of the poor nations and of the destitute in our own society is their own fault. It is sad when free enterprise worshippers become as dogmatic and callous as the most doctrinaire Marxist. Indian poet Rabindranath Tagore once commented, "God is ashamed when the prosperous boast of his special favor."

There is corruption just as there are scroungers. But at times we seem to want to use these exceptions to fault other people's compassionate efforts, perhaps as a justification for not doing anything ourselves. I couldn't help comparing some things said about hunger with myths that are spread about the history of Ireland and which were put into perspective by the words of an English Bishop: "We need to say: 'Forget the myths, because the truth is bad enough.' "

The truth is that hunger is growing, at home and abroad. Though for now I will focus on Oregon. More than 10% of the Oregon work force is without jobs. Many families that have never before known financial hardship are exhausting their savings and their unemployment compensation as well as the capacity of family and friends to support them. Some are without money, food and shelter. They are losing self-esteem and hope. More than 100,000 households in the state are counted officially as living in poverty; 54,860 people used up 26 weeks of unemployment benefit and 46,025 the extended 13-week program as well, with another 35,000 having received at least one payment of this extended program.

These figures are provided by Oregon Food Share which is a network of 350 emergency food organizations which reaches needy Oregonians in every county. Its Director, Kathleen Cornett, tells me that Oregon is the first to have a complete statewide network for moving food that also includes rural areas. She reports a dramatic increase in requests for help in the past two years as do the various religious agencies with whom I have talked. The volunteer agencies which receive the food from Oregon Food Share now operate 50 on-site meal programs serving more than a million households. In 1983 nearly 70,000 volunteer hours went into distributing eight million pounds of food. In the current year she predicts that nine and a half million pounds of food will be needed to serve more than 15 million meals, the equivalent of feeding every Oregonian for two days. The scale of gifts and the work of volunteers enables costs to be kept to a minimum — fourteen cents per food basket meal and $1.84 for a household. The budget for providing emergency food services this year is one and a half million dollars.

Oregon Food Share welcomes donations of food as well as

money. Every day gifts arrive at its capacious Portland warehouse ranging from fish from Newport to Idaho potatoes. They may come from individuals or companies. Safeway, for instance, gives the leftovers from all their stores. This is also the distribution point for government food like cheese and flour. Those who would like to donate food or money or time can reach Oregon Food Share at 3939 SE 26th, Portland, Oregon 97202. The telephone number is (503) 239-1010. Farmers, commercial growers and storeowners are eligible for a tax write-off.

One last statistic: It is estimated that every Oregonian wastes 246 pounds of food every year. Or, put in another way, 640 million pounds of food is thrown away by the whole State annually. To grow that wasted food took 10,600,000 barrels of oil, 400,000 pounds of fertilizer, and 1,500,000 acres of arable land. Kathleen Cornett says, "Please think of us when you see food being wasted."

March 22, 1984

Presidential election

WELL, IT'S ALL OVER: except, of course, for the computer analysts who have many well-paid days before them assessing what this or that swing meant and whether Geraldine Ferraro's historic nomination made a difference and why the Italian men of Queens voted the way they did. Amost everyone will breathe a sigh of relief that the seemingly interminable campaign is behind us. We can enjoy a slight letup in political pollsters sampling us over the telephone or pundits pontificating from electronic pulpits. No more League of Women Voters-hosted debates for a while or propositions to be confused by and, as the rain and the wind do their job, fewer tattered signs on telephone poles and vacant lots to remind us of what might have been. As Will Rogers said, fifty years ago, commenting on the way politicians predict disaster if their opponents are elected, "I don't think we will be ruined next Tuesday, no matter who is elected, so the politicians will have to wait four more years to tell us who will ruin us then."

A lot of people are rejoicing at the result. A lot are downhearted. The disappointment after such hard work is great. The public has spoken. Though I know some who would agree with De Tocqueville when he said, "Universal suffrage is by no means a guarantee of the wisdom of the popular choice."

An Indian politician once defined democracy for me with the words, "The batting side can be made to field." If he had been with me as I stayed up to watch the election results in Washington, DC yesterday, he might have added, "Or be given a second innings."

Elections are a precious asset. Freedom House estimates that only one in three of the world's population gets the chance to vote in a genuinely free election. Some here may look at four years with some dismay, but spare a thought for most of the globe's inhabitants who see little prospect of the batting side ever being made to field. I was struck by the enthusiasm of a Soviet refugee who cast her first vote in an American election this week. Eva Rabinovich comes from Latvia and has been a US citizen less than two months. "In the Soviet Union," she is quoted in the *Washington Post,* "we were told who to vote for, so why bother. But now we are the free people. We make a real vote." Describing the sensation of going into the polling booth, she said, "It sort of gives me the shake in the knees. My friend Yara and I keep talking about it, that we, just peons, will pick the President of the United States of America."

Elections do not always bring out the best in the politicians or in us. All that does credit to us or our case is marshalled skillfully. All that discredits or is inconvenient is suppressed. Few set out to campaign with the philosophy of the dockers in Brazil who introduced free elections for the first time in their port of Rio. "The way we conduct these elections," they announced, "is as important as winning them."

Reagan's triumph has been earned. He will go down in history as the President with the largest electoral landslide in American politics. But no leader worth his jellybeans would be satisfied with a *Guinness Book of World Records*-type statistic. Is it too visionary to hope that he might be recorded as the peacekeeper of the twentieth century? No longer the recruiting sergeant of the unilateralists, as he was dubbed in Europe in his first term, could

he become the man who removed the spectre of nuclear incinera-
tion which bugs our children? With an overwhelming personal
mandate and a beefed-up defense and a united nation behind him
he could afford to go the extra mile walk in the woods with the
Russian Bear.

Would it be too visionary, too, to hope that by his actions he
could be perceived by his most virulent critics as president of all
the people of the United States? Not having to worry about defending his policies in a reelection could he become the champion
of those who can least defend themselves, and do it with the
sensitivity and sincerity his wife is bringing to the world of drug
abuse?

Of course he *is* the President of all the people as was so
movingly expressed by Fritz Mondale in his gracious speech
acknowledging defeat. In a curious way it is three different remarks by the losing candidate which stick in my mind from these
elections. During the second presidential debate Mondale said
something like, "I respect your commitment to peace, President
Reagan. I hope you will respect mine to strength." It needed to be
said and believed. Again I was impressed and slightly amused by
two answers Mondale gave to *Newsweek* questions. "If you win,"
he was asked, "what will you say about America and its values in
1984?" He replied, "That we are a practical, just, caring and
peaceful people." "And if you lose?" "That we are a practical,
just, caring and peaceful people." Then lastly the concession
speech. I hope the President watched it or has read it. It was not
easy for Mondale to make even if he had probably realized for
some while the inevitable. In a way the sad thing about the night
was that he had moved beyond his supporters in his generosity to
Reagan. They booed when he said, "He has won. We are all
Americans. He is our President. We honor him tonight." The
choice had been made by the American people with dignity and
majesty, he said, and "although I would rather have won tonight
we rejoice in our democracy, we rejoice in the freedom of a
wonderful people, and we accept their verdict." Now for the sake
of the poor, the unemployed, the elderly, the handicapped, the
helpless and the sad the struggle had to continue.

"Let us fight for jobs and fairness. Let us fight for these kids and make certain they've had the best education that any genera-tion ever had. Let us fight for our environment and protect our air, our water and our land. And while we must keep America strong, let's use that strength to keep the peace, to reflect our values and to control these weapons before they destroy us all. That has been my fight . . . and we must fight for those goals with all of our heart in the future."

Such graciousness in defeat elevates the quality of public life for all.

I saw another example on TV last week in a quite different setting. It was as unexpected and inspiring as it was untypical. There was a professional soccer match being strongly contested by two top teams. A player was injured. An opponent noticed this and, to stop play, booted the ball out. When the player had been attended to, the player's teammate, as was his right, was given the ball to restart the game. He promptly threw it in — to his oppo-nent.

Politics, sport, life — it is up to each of us to set the tone.

November 8, 1984

Common language

MY FAVORITE BUMPERSTICKER, which I observed on a freeway outside Washington, DC, is "Eschew obfuscation." Which, I suppose, is a roundabout reminder to say things clearly. Or as my dictionary would put it "to shun that which obscures clarity." My daughter, aged 10, would seem to be a master of this art. To her things are either gross or they're awesome, she's either stuffed or she's starving. She eschews obfuscation with the same effortless-ness as she chews gum.

In my commentary this morning I want to strike a more serious note than usual. I want to talk about the English language and the difficulties of communication which an Englishman faces when he comes to a country where according to the song in *My Fair Lady* "they haven't spoken it for years." No, that isn't fair, is it? Some people, perhaps rightly, claim that some American English is closer to what they used to speak in England than what today passes for the Queen's English. It is certainly different. And this applies not only to the meaning of individual words but to the whole approach to the use of language.

Let me give you an example which illustrates the switch of mentality that is required. It is a true story about a Dutch friend of mine, Frits Philips, who was head of a multi-national electrical firm based in Eindhoven. At the end of World War II conditions in Holland which had been occupied by the Germans were serious. There was a terrible shortage of food and the calorie intake of the population in Eindhoven was down to 600, less than during the occupation. Philips drove to Paris to discuss the situation with officers at SHAEF, the Allied Headquarters. With some difficulty he got through to the British general in charge. Now Philips knew that one does not always get far with the British by overdramatic language. So, after some small talk, when he was asked how the food supply was in Eindhoven, Philips replied, "Not good, really." There was silence for a moment, then the general said, "Is it as bad as that?" Soon a column of lorries, sorry, trucks, was on its way from Normandy to Eindhoven with supplies of food for the Dutch people. Somehow I can't imagine Governor Atiyeh getting very far if he tried that approach with President Reagan.

Subtle suggestion and studied understatement just don't get across in a land attuned to the hard sell. I have noticed in that regard that if you play down your own abilities here, people will take you at your word. Supposing someone in England, for instance, were to ask me if I played soccer well. If I replied, "Not too bad," I would be thought even boastful. That answer here would not get you into the starting lineup.

Some of the straightforward differences of language are pretty well known: sidewalk not pavement, candy not sweets, dessert not pudding, trunk not boot of your car, hood not bonnet, freeway not motorway, aluminum not aluminium. And my daughter's see-saw is now a teeter-totter. It's an elevator and not a lift and, by the way, it's useful for an Englishman to discover early on that if you get in on the ground floor and press the button for 1 you're not going up in the world. In England the first floor is the American second floor.

Sporting language is a credit course in itself. You'll fairly quickly be able to distinguish the 6-pack from the Pac-10 or even the Portapak. But no sooner have you learned to appreciate a slamdunk, than you have to move on and know about RBI's and the fact that a doubleheader is not someone in Ripley's *Believe It Or Not*. Then before long you are into sacks and blitzes which have nothing to do with Fifth Avenue or the Germans.

You've got to keep up with the latest Americanese too. I remember when I first arrived I asked a lady what she did. She told me she was teaching a Vietnamese to verbalize in a one to one situation. I figured out eventually that in the old English to which I was accustomed she was giving private tutoring in English. In these modern times, of course, people don't understand you anyway, they read you. And if they fail to read you you have to run it by them again.

And now that I'm beginning to get the hang of Oregon I wonder how it will be in other parts of the United States. As a small boy I was evacuated during World War II to New England where I lived for five years before returning to England. My father came over to America at one point for a few days and visited me in Boston. Wanting to unbend a bit and make allowance for the American language, he said, "I suppose you find things *swell* here." Apparently I, aged 10, corrected him, "Daddy, we don't say *swell* in Boston."

Well, have a good day, as they say, and be sure to eschew obfuscation, remember to take your sack for the brownbagger, oh and a last piece of advice, do hug your frog.

You know, if I were ever to write a revue about life here I would entitle it, "America will return, after these messages."

September 23, 1982

Pasadena

AS PORTLAND starts a new year and a new administration I
thought I would pass on some news about a significant initiative
in another City of Roses, Pasadena. Particularly as it involves
citizen input, a priority of our new Mayor, Bud Clark.

Having a population of only 120,000, Pasadena's experience
may not be entirely relevant to our city but its spirit certainly is. It
shows what one committed individual can achieve by listening to
people's concerns.

It all began in August 1983 when educator Denise Wood
undertook a task commissioned by her church: to make a survey
of the quality of life of Pasadena and then to write a report which
could be the church's centennial gift to the city.

She bought a tape recorder and started to interview citizens,
one on one, sometimes several times. She did this eight hours a
day for nine months, listening to a good crosssection of the city.
People confided their deepest fears and thoughts because she was
not trying to put anything across. "Having a few grey hairs
helped," she says. She studied reports, attended hearings, read
press articles.

What she found may have surprised those who consider
Pasadena a most livable city; she found a community in pain. An
outward face to the world of the Tournament of Roses concealed
the reality of rampant crime and poverty as a daily fact of life.

At the end of her time of listening she produced a 53-page
report. It analyzed in detail the problems, with facts, statistics,
and the human anguish she had encountered. It also described
"green shoots," areas where despair was turning to hope, and
noted existing resources the city could enlist for tackling community problems in a coordinated way.

This comprehensive summary included details of the disinte-
gration of family life and an incidence of reported child abuse that
has gone up 500% in two years, and of the struggle for survival
by many, especially the elderly, the young, Hispanics and blacks.
It recorded the fact that 21% of elementary schoolchildren were
from families receiving payments from Aid to Families with De-

pendent Children and 54% qualified for food and reduced payment lunch programs. It pictured a community where demand for welfare services, food and hospitality is increasing alarmingly, and where sub-standard housing means that 20 people are using one toilet and 12 people sharing one room; a community where drug and alcohol abuse has reached an all time high and where there is inequality between blacks and whites in employment and unemployment.

Under "green shoots" Denise listed 15 organizations made up of people who didn't wait for others but rolled up their sleeves and went to work. These ranged from the Armenian Oral History Project to the Mexican-American Scholarship Fund, from the Community Dispute Resolution Center to the Contact Crisis Counselling Hotline. "Their results," she says, "were born from the qualities of the people involved far more than the amount of money being spent. Individuals and their care and courage and leadership were what made the crucial difference." Among these growth points was the Community Skills Center in which her husband John is involved. There, young people and adults are trained in job entry skills linked to the area job market. It is run jointly by the city, the city college and the school district. It serves 3500 students annually. Tuition-free training is provided as well as counseling and help with finding jobs. According to a school board member it has become a symbol of cooperation and caring.

The chief concerns of her report are not to allow Pasadena to become a polarized city, one part rich, one part poor, and to make the quality of life of all Pasadena young people everybody's business. The Rev. Wilbur Johnson, former head of the Ministerial Alliance and now Advisor to the City Manager, told Denise, "Your report will get results. There was no name-calling, no blame, yet you have not watered down the facts."

As Denise went round the city she found she had been "connecting people," as she calls it, that the city was as disconnected as it was divided. For instance, she told us, there were 192 social agencies, all doing good work, but these professionals had not sat down together in the same room. Few people were thinking for the whole city. So she had proposed in her report that an Office for Creative Connections be set up. "My basic feeling," she says, "is that if you connect people they have within them the seeds of the solution."

That Office is now operational, with Denise as its Director. Its mandate: to continue this process of listening; to make the connections between individuals and groups who by better understanding each other can make a difference in resolving the city's problems; to speak out on the vital concerns of the report; and to encourage programs and enterprises that will improve the city's livability.

"None of us alone can assure that our city will not become permanently divided, polarized," she wrote in her report. "Working together, over the long haul, we can. None of us alone can protect our own and others' children from some of the ravages of the modern age. Together, with the help of the young people, we can find creative ways to move into a new social climate."

Perhaps every city should have an Office for Creative Connections.

January 10, 1985

Return of the Indian spirit

THIS PAST WEEK we had in Portland the visit of a husband and wife book publishing team, Bill and Phyl Cameron Johnson. Phyl is the editor and is an American and Bill is the illustrator and English. Those of you who listen to KBOO's Indian World program on Monday nights will have heard them interviewed by John Talley. For the Cameron Johnsons have just brought out a book called *Return of the Indian Spirit,* published by Celestial Arts of Millbrae, California. The book is in three parts: first, a story, Return of the Indian Spirit by Vinson Brown; second, the Laws of the Lodge and the Wisdom of the Old Ones; and third, a selection inspired by Chief Seattle's speech of surrender in 1855 and an Indian prayer. *The Circle,* the American Indian newspaper in Minneapolis, describing the book as a remarkably eloquent story, writes, "People of different colors and ages may come to love and cherish this book for its moral values and wisdom of the Indian way past and present."

I asked Phyl Cameron Johnson how it was that a white couple thousands of miles away in London could produce a book with this Indian theme and do so in a way that won the confidence and even endorsement of native Americans.

Phyl replied with two stories. As a young girl growing up in Illinois her grade school had had the foresight to include each year a visit by a band of Navajo Indians who would set up their traditional way of life in the school gymnasium. The schoolchildren, ages six and seven, were encouraged to spend a lot of time with them. Thus Phyl grew up with a great love and almost reverence for Indian culture. One particular bit of Indian philosophy had influenced her whole life: always tell the truth. Indeed, some of the Indian lore gathered in her book is a challenge to all cultures: every man must treat with respect all such things as are sacred to other people whether he comprehends them or not. Or this chant from the Osages:

> When you arise in the morning
> Give thanks for the morning light.
> Give thanks for your life and strength
> Give thanks for your food
> And give thanks for the joy of living.
> And if perchance you see no reason
>   for giving thanks,
> Rest assured the fault is in yourself.

Phyl's second deep experience was in her twenties as a teacher in a school in Northern Michigan. The children were largely of Indian background but had been made to feel so ashamed of their heritage that they did not want to admit it and knew next to nothing about it. Phyl recounts how inadequate the text books were. On one occasion she came to a section in a social studies book which said that the Indian did not know how to look after his land until the white man came and taught him to cut down trees and mine for minerals. She was ashamed and recognised even thirty years ago how perverted this judgement was. It was clear even then, she says, that we had gone a long way in defiling

Mother Nature. She would quickly skip over such bits in the text books and hope the children didn't notice them.

In the course of time through her sensitivity she was able to help many of the children identify with the greatness of their race. And these experiences years ago stirred in her the wish to do something practical to restore respect for moral and spiritual values among children everywhere. She began with research on the Indians and found, among other things, how much Washington and Franklin had been impressed with the democratic roots of the Iroquois Indians and had some of the experience of the Iroquois Confederacy of Peace written into the American Constitution.

In the book's dedication she writes of the American Indian children: "Their heritage of enduring values has often given me the courage I needed to tackle the difficult decisions in my life with confidence." She says that their culture had inspired her to live outside herself — and that a people who live outside themselves have something very precious in today's disintegrating society. The time has come, she adds, when the best of every culture is needed to sustain every other culture. She had started with the indigenous culture she knew best. In this task she had the help of her husband who had lived for a time on Indian reservations in New Mexico and Alberta and had filled his sketch pad with drawings. The result is *Return of the Indian Spirit.*

This week has been officially designated Oregon Indian Week and I conclude with the prayer of Tom Whitecloud which comes at the end of the book:

O Great Spirit

Whose voice I hear in the winds
And whose breath gives life
To all the world,
Hear me. I am a man before you.
One of your many children.
I am small and weak.
I need your strength and wisdom.

Let me walk in beauty.
And make my eyes ever behold
The red and purple sunset.
Make my hands respect
The things you have made,
My ears sharp to hear your voice.

Make me wise, so that I may know
The things you have taught my people,
The lessons you have hidden
In every leaf and rock.

I seek strength,
Not to be superior to my brothers
But to be able to fight
My greatest enemy, myself.

Make me ever ready to come to you,
With clean hands and straight eye,
So when life fades as the fading sunset
My spirit may come to you without shame.

May 27, 1982

6 The Soviet Union and us

Two conferences

A SENIOR GROUP of Soviet officials recently visited Portland. Did we miss the chance to tell them what we feel about the suppression of human rights in their country? Did we betray those in the Soviet Union who appeal to us for help? I don't know. But some people feel that out of politeness or out of fear of exacerbating the situation between our two countries in a way that could bring war nearer, we refrain from speaking up when we should.

There were two conferences the same week in Portland in February. One at Lewis and Clark College, attended by those Soviet officials, was on US-Soviet relations, the other at Reed College on "Two Faces of Soviet Reality: Religious Repression and Anti-semitism."

At Lewis and Clark the emphasis was on finding common interests in a dangerous world. Areas of disagreement seemed to be consciously kept to a minimum. Human rights were hardly mentioned, at least publicly, and even when events in Afghanistan were described or the suggestion made that such a conference be held in Moscow without KGB involvement, some people I talked with said that they were embarrassed and that it was rude to our distinguished Soviet guests.

At Reed the 150 people who met were dealing specifically with abuses of human rights. They met against a backdrop of 100 names of Soviet prisoners who had appealed to the West for help. The conference was co-sponsored by the American Jewish Committee and Ecumenical Ministries of Oregon. How to assure global survival and advance human rights was the foreign policy issue which most frequently confounded the experts, Senator Mark Hatfield pointed out at the religious conference.

Whereas earlier in the week coexistence had been put forward by the Soviet delegation as the linchpin of their foreign policy, Senator Hatfield stated, "Ultimate coexistence is impossible between religion and Soviet ideology." While a Soviet official had condemned the use of trade as an instrument of politics, the Senator said that the US should utilize its economic power as a bargaining chip. "When we talk wheat," he said, "the Russians talk turkey, or emigration." He went on to urge the US to "clean up its own act" if it wanted credibility in dealing with the Soviets, and to pursue quiet, carefully prepared approaches on human rights.

At both conferences participants urged restraint on rhetoric. "There are so many good people in Russia, we must be careful how we use words and assess evils," said Sister Ann Gillen, Executive Director of the National Interreligious Task Force on Soviet Jewry. At the same time we had to realize that organized hatred in an enclosed society would lead to a *pogrom,* she said, speaking of anti-semitism which was increasing in the USSR. 263,000 Jews and 50,000 Christians had been allowed to leave the country but "now the doors are shut and we need a miracle to open them again."

Dr. Kent Hill, Professor of Russian History at Seattle Pacific University, said that we were "buying the Soviet line" if we failed to tackle human rights because of nuclear dangers. "If we are paralyzed about fear of our own extinction," he said, "we will never speak out on behalf of anyone." It was also naive, he added, to assume that silence would buy lack of danger. Professor Hill said that he had talked in Moscow with church leaders. On their return from visits to the US they had, like the officials visiting Lewis and Clark, to report on their trip. These leaders had asked him, "Why did you treat us so well and not criticize our system?"

I was not surprised to hear the Russian visitors to Lewis and Clark say that the Soviet Union went into Afghanistan because "we were cornered by the Americans," that they were still there because "the US has done everything not to allow us to extricate ourselves," that Cuban troops were in Angola to protect American oilworkers, that America was the closed society. But I was surprised to meet audience members who took at face value the words of a Soviet diplomat, "I am not speaking for my government but presenting my views" and were upset with me for not believing that the Soviet group were pure academics.

The President of Lewis and Clark College, Dr. James Gardner, had the balance right when, welcoming the Russians, he said that we needed to be tough-minded but warm-hearted. There is certainly nothing to be gained by rudeness or, as one participant in the Reed College conference suggested, treating the Russians with contempt. In fact, I apologized publicly to the Russians at the World Affairs Council lunch for the disgraceful bomb attack at the New York embassy residence the day before.

All the same, bearing in mind what was said at the Reed conference, I can't help wondering whether the report by the Russians will accurately reflect what people here feel. I am conscious of wars that started at least in part because dictators miscalculated the depths of feeling of peoples about human rights.

April 2, 1984

Strength and weakness

MILLIONS OF WORDS must have winged their way by satellite around the world about Korean flight 007 and the recriminations which seem to follow endlessly on that tragedy. However, eight words on the cover of the British news magazine *The Economist,* along with an inset of Andropov and a picture of the plane, seem to me the most telling comment out of all the rest. *The Economist* cover simply said, "You had nothing to lose by saying sorry."

The world would certainly be sleeping more restfully if they had.

Few people now recall that in 1955 the Bulgarians shot down an El Al Constellation killing 58 people. Or that only ten years ago in 1973 the Israelis destroyed a Libyan Boeing over the Sinai killing 104 people. The Bulgarians apologized. The Israelis, after first trying to justify their action, invited in Arab investigators and even paid some compensation, although they didn't call it that.

The wrongs had been done just as surely as over the Sea of Okhotsk, the mistakes had been made, the innocent had suffered. But the tragedy was not compounded by such callous disregard for facts and the threat to do it again. Nor did ideological opponents make such a meal over the incidents as some are doing today. Ironically, the Soviet newsagency Tass did condemn the downing of the Libyan jet as an "impudent and wicked act of aggression."

The truth is that we all make terrible mistakes—and respond to sincere apology when it is offered.

To Westerners, lying does seem to be the chief among sins. In the Watergate saga it was Nixon's coverup rather than the burglary and the underhand methods which seemed most to disturb the inhabitants of this free society. In Britain the public was far more dismayed that Profumo, Secretary of State for War, had lied to the House of Commons than that he had been involved with a callgirl and a Soviet naval attaché. And long may this veneration for truth continue. It is the guarantee of the survival of democracy.

At the same time for Soviet leaders such moral outrage is probably incomprehensible. As Conor Cruise O'Brien wrote in *The Observer* last month, "They started lying as a matter of historic necessity. They went on lying as a matter of institutional necessity. By now they have reached the point where, if they stopped lying, their country would fall apart."

But if it is so hard for the Soviets to say sorry, it may be reason for us not to make it harder for them to do so. I do not imagine their human nature is very different from ours. None of us like to have our mistakes spotlighted by others. I remember that when Britain attacked Suez I felt very ashamed. But as Britain became more and more the focus of world opprobrium I felt less and less like apologizing. I know, too, that some of my South African friends who are very critical of their regime at home, sometimes outspokenly and courageously so, meet such intemperate criticism of their country when they are overseas that they soon find themselves springing to its defense.

I felt that I should apologize this week for something an organization I was involved in had been remiss about which affected another group of people. The fact that the others may have been more at fault did not make it less right to put our side right. I once heard an Italian senator say, "Even if you are only ten percent in the wrong you must start by admitting where you are in the wrong." As it happened the other people apologized in turn to us and the basis was laid for working together.

Of course, it is important that apologies are made because they are due and made sincerely. I remember playing in a game of field hockey. A teammate got so fed up he clouted the opposing goal-keeper with his stick. Knowing my friend and hearing that he had apologized, I asked him if he had really meant it. He replied, "No, but it was the decent thing to do."

I am not suggesting for a moment that we do anything to soften the prickings of conscience which, suppress them as they may try to do, still must afflict the Soviet leadership. I do not share the view that somehow our words are responsible for their bullets. The differences between a free society and a Communist society have been made transparent to the world and I am glad that this is so. Yet once this distinction has been drawn we may need a modicum of modesty about our own society.

Recently I interviewed a white couple from Africa. Her father had been buried alive by the Mau Mau in Kenya. She refused to let bitterness and blame into her life. That was extraordinary enough. But I was also struck by a further truth expressed by her husband. They had gone beyond forgiving, he said, to "facing where we as whites were responsible for the tragedy — our arro-gance, our selfishness, the way we dominated."

Communism grew out of the failure of so-called Christian societies to live in the revolutionary way Christ intended. Recog-nition of that fact might give us more chance of changing the Russians. Certainly a more humble approach will be needed with the Chinese if, as I read in *The Oregonian* last week, one of the things dividing our nations is the "bitter memories that Chinese of all political stripes carry of foreign domination from the middle of the 19th century to the middle of the 20th century."

I have a feeling that the demise of Communism will be has-tened by a more passionate commitment to remedy our own weaknesses as much as by a crusade for democracy and a surfeit of fingerpointing.

George Washington's words in his farewell address might even have some relevance in the present situation: "The nation which indulges toward another an habitual hatred or an habitual fondness is in some degree a slave. It is a slave to its animosity or to its affection, either of which is sufficient to lead it astray from its duty and its interest. Antipathy in one nation against another disposes each more readily to offer insult and injury, to lay hold of slight causes of umbrage, and to be haughty and intractable when accidental or trifling occasions of dispute occur."

October 13, 1983

Andrei Sakharov

I DON'T KNOW if you have noticed but there is an extraordinary mix of Soviet-related events this week in Portland. On Wednesday a US-Soviet conference began at Lewis and Clark College with senior Soviet officials taking part. The same day the Soviet emigré orchestra made its local debut. This top class ensemble consists largely of musicians from Soviet symphony orchestras. Then this weekend there is a conference at Reed College on religious repression and anti-semitism in the Soviet Union.

This would seem an appropriate moment to draw attention to an urgent appeal by Nobel Peace Prize winner, Andrei Sakharov.

Sakharov's name will be familiar to most people. In the '60s he was known as the father of the Soviet hydrogen bomb. In the '70s he became, writes Norwegian artist, Victor Sparre, "the father of all who suffer persecution in the Soviet Union." From being the youngest Academician, a holder of the Order of Lenin, winner of the Stalin Prize, three times a Hero of Socialist Labor, he became the Soviet Union's best known dissident. He was asked to give back all his awards. His Nobel Peace Prize citation described him as a "spokesman for the conscience of mankind."

Over the years Sakharov developed doubts about the morality of building nuclear weapons. In 1962 he asked Khrushchev not to proceed with tests, he donated the money he had earned from nuclear work to a cancer hospital, and he began to be regarded as a critic of the regime.

Nuclear dangers are still his concern. He has warned that an all-out nuclear war could mean the destruction of contemporary civilization, even cause the annihilation of life on earth. He sees nuclear weapons only making sense as a means of deterring nuclear aggression by a potential enemy.

In a major essay in *Foreign Affairs* last year he says that in attempting not to lag behind a potential enemy, we condemn ourselves to an arms race that is tragic. But if the danger of slipping into an all-out nuclear war can be reduced at the cost of another 10 or 15 years of the arms race, he writes, then perhaps the price must be paid, while, at the same time, diplomatic, economic, ideological, political, cultural, and social efforts are made to prevent a war.

The Soviet scientist says that he shares the yearnings in the West for a peaceful solution to world problems. But, he continues, "It is absolutely necessary to be mindful of the specific political, military, and strategic realities of the present day and to do so objectively without making any sort of allowances for either side; this also means that one should not proceed from an *a priori* assumption of any special peace-loving nature in the Socialist countries due to their supposed progressiveness or the horrors and losses they have experienced in war."

For nearly eighteen years, as well as singling out the dangers of nuclear war, Sakharov has also spoken out for victims of repression. He was a co-founder of the Moscow Human Rights Committee. "Every time I see an injustice done to one of my fellow men," he says, "I must and I will speak up."

Sakharov is today in Gorky. He is, as Jerome Shestack, President of the International League for Human Rights, says, "forced to live in exile, harrassed by police agents, denied the solace of family, children and colleagues and deprived of freedom and dignity."

His safety, in so far as it exists, depends on the watchful eyes of his friends in the West. Such support helped end the press campaign against him in 1973 and drew attention to his hunger strike in 1981 which won permission for his daughter-in-law to join her husband in the US. Appeals by the US Academy of Sciences may have saved his life. "Write of us," Sakharov told a friend of mine. "We beg you to. That is our best defense."

Sixty-two and suffering from a heart condition, Sakharov is

deprived of adequate medical assistance, banned from corresponding with or talking to foreigners, even from personal communications with his children and grandchildren. Government spokesmen have even begun to start describing him as "cuckoo." But Sakharov's appeal is not on behalf of himself but for his wife, Elena, who, he believes, is in greater danger. For many years she and her family have been the victims of a campaign of smears and pressures. Now that the younger members have emigrated, he writes, his wife is "the sole hostage for my public activity." The KGB had sought to eliminate her moral influence and, he adds, he had reason to fear, her physical presence as well. "Even if I am exaggerating the danger, the public harrassment and constant KGB interference precludes any possibility for serious medical treatment."

Elena, herself a medical doctor who was badly wounded as a nurse in the war, asked for an exit visa in September 1982 when an urgent eye operation was needed. Her eyes still require treatment but her heart disease now has priority. Sakharov wrote personally to Andropov on this matter but received no answer. He also appealed this January to the European Security conference. She has had no reply to her visa application. "I appeal to my colleagues abroad and in the USSR, to public figures and government figures in all countries, to our friends everywhere. Save my wife, Elena Bonner," writes Sakharov.

I spoke to Elena's daughter, Tanya, earlier this week. She tells me that her mother has suffered two heart attacks and that only in the West can she have the kind of bypass surgery she needs.

If the new Soviet ruler, Konstantin Chernenko, wants to place US-USSR relations on a more healthy basis, as he apparently intimated to Vice-President Bush, he could hardly do better than to make a start by giving Elena Bonner a chance of health.

As Elena says, "We cannot achieve peace in the world through hate, only through caring for people. We must tell the truth about oppression and suffering, but we must seek a new way to live together."

February 23, 1984

Anti-Communism

I WANT TODAY to tackle what I believe is one of the greatest weaknesses in our present foreign political attitudes and that is anti-Communism. I would suggest that anti-Communism has contributed more than pro-Communism to the spread of Communism in the world. Most of the countries that are Communist became Communist because of the actions of history's greatest anti-Communist, Adolph Hitler. And on the current world scene probably the biggest weapon in the armory of Communism is the racial situation in the most outspokenly anti-Communist country, South Africa.

Now, lest I be misunderstood, let me quickly add that I feel very strongly that Communism is wrong, that it poses a threat to democracy and is a retrograde step for mankind. Its economic theories are discredited and its ideology has lost the power to inspire commitment. I am also in favor of a powerful military defence to deter the aggression of Communist countries which is nowadays fired less by ideological zeal than by old-fashioned power politics. The principal superiority of democracy over Communism, in my view, is the value we place on the individual and the fact that in our system people have the chance to remove their leaders if they are not satisfied with them.

But, if there were one single recognition which could transform our policies today — and incidentally moderate the stridency of the so-called Moral Majority — it would be if we faced up to the fact that Communism exists because of the failure of us Christians through the years to take Christ's demands seriously and deal with injustice around us. If we accepted that premise we might still feel the need for a sure defence but we might have more humility in our approach to Communist countries, more understanding of what makes Communists tick and a bit of vision for what they could become.

Thirty years ago Tom Keep, a docker, a longshoreman, who was a friend of our family and had been a longtime Communist leader in the London docks, visited the United States . He had a meeting in Washington with Senators and Congressmen. They plied him with questions. They asked him why he had become a Communist. "I had a daughter," he replied. "She did not get enough to eat because we were too poor. She died. That evening a priest came to my home and prayed with me and said that the girl would be buried without charge. Later in the evening the Communists came and said, 'Stick with us and we'll smash the system.' I joined the party that night."

The legislators asked him all about his training in Communism. He told them he had been taught to use money and sex to corrupt and win individuals and had promoted jealousy and hatred to foster division. He also described how he had changed and how his family had been reunited and had returned to the Catholic church. At the end of the long evening the Senators said, "Good night." The longshoreman cut in. "Just a moment. You have asked me many questions. Can I ask you one or two?" They were surprised but agreed. "You have all talked a lot about Communism tonight," he said. "How many of you have ever sat down with one Communist and changed him?" There was no answer. He then said, "How many of you know how to sit down with a difficult person who is not a Communist and change him?" Again, no answer. "When democracy learns that secret," he said, "democracy will win the world."

There is a provocative perspective on Communism in Peter Howard's play *Mr. Brown Comes Down the Hill*. This is an attempt to visualize what might happen if Christ came to earth today. In one scene Mr. Brown, who is Christ, is cross-questioned on his views by a group of bishops who are suspicious of his theology. One of them says his ideas are Communism. "Communism?" says Mr. Brown. "D'you know, that's a word that's been used more and more and means less and less, like Fascism. It's a dirty word from people who don't understand it. Look here, you bishops. Look, put yourselves up in the skies, if you've the imagination to do it. Imagine yourself up there, looking down on this torn, suffering, amazing planet, to judge it if you can, to show mercy as you must, to pity and punish as you dare. Imagine the millions of hearts and faces turned up to you there in hope and prayer. Imagine the millions of backs turned away from you in disillusionment and hatred. Here are the Communists teeming

over half the earth. Now, from their mother's milk they've been
fed Karl Marx. They've been taught to hate God. They've no
knowledge of him except by stealth and instinct. They've mur-
dered him, or done their best to do it. But they've marched
through sweat and toil and misery to feed the hungry, to house the
homeless, to put hope of something new into the hearts of humanity. Then here are the non-Communists with their strong
sense of their own righteousness. They talk about God. Some of
them even print 'In God we trust' on their money. But out of this
half of the earth, for all their protestations and opportunities, have
come two world wars in fifty years, the castor oil of Fascism, the
gas chambers and Gestapo of Hitler, and the toleration of social
and economic injustices that gave Marx his philosophy and Stalin
his fuel and flame. They've been taught to fear God, but all they
do is flee from him. Now you have the Christian West glorifying
sex and satirizing faith — rationalizing the materialism they de-
spise and hate in their enemies. They've had the wealth. They've
had the power. They've had the chance of faith. They've been
entrusted, so they say, with the hope and truth of all ages. But
what have they done with it?''

I think of that question when I see China opening up to the
West. What attitudes, what lifestyle will they get from us? I ask
myself, supposing instead of a clamp-down in Poland there were
an opening to us, would we be ready? We have been entrusted, so
we say, with the hope and truth of all ages, what will we do with it
now?

January 7, 1982

7 My home town

Scrubbing London

WHENEVER I SEE that popular American raincoat "London fog" I think how inappropriate the name is, how it perpetuates a false image of my home town. Rain, yes, fog, no. At least the pea-souper, stock in trade of thrillers and period descriptions of the British capital, is a thing of the past. I remember in the late '40s when someone had to walk in front of a bus, like in the wartime blackout, to guide it through the gloom. I recall a famous soccer match between Arsenal and Moscow Dynamo when no one, even the referee, could see both goalposts or all the players. Photos taken twenty years ago still record murky figures groping in the smog, faces covered by scarves or masks to keep out chemicals and dirt. For older people the air could be life-threatening. But London fog ain't what it used to be; not because of any climatic changes but because of human decision.

By the middle of the last century, thanks to the industrial re-volution, much of Britain's air was smoky and acrid, and rivers were being choked to death by industrial effluent and domestic sewage. In 1848 and 1863 Parliament enacted measures to control freshwater and air pollution — and environmentalism was born. But in this century, with the further expansion of the railway network—London has six major stations—and the advent of the motor car and truck, and the enormous growth in population, pollution threatened to get out of hand. In the 1950's environ-mental concern led to increased government regulation.

As a result, between 1958 and 1960 the length of tidal and non-tidal rivers and canals in England and Wales classed as grossly polluted fell from 7% to 2½% of total length. Partly due to the Clean Air Acts of 1956 to 1968, partly from a switch to cleaner fuels like natural gas, the emission of smoke has been cut back over 85%. Sulphur Dioxide emissions have been reduced by a third since 1970. There have been impressive achievements, too, in areas as diverse as land reclamation and the phasing out of dangerous pesticides.

Concern for the environment is most evident to the eye in the cleaning of London. In 1981, for instance, the Property Services Agency began a six million dollar rolling program to repair, restore and conserve the external stonework of the Houses of Parliament, one of the 2000 buildings of architectural and historical importance which this Department of the Environment Agency maintains. The work is done by using low-pressure, low-volume jets of water and hand scrubbing with bristle and phosphorous brushes. Now much of Parliament, like Westminster Abbey, stands out in elegant cream stone in contrast to the dirty brown of the uncleaned part.

Roger Bush, Principal Information Officer at the agency, tells me that this spring the Big Ben Clock Tower should emerge from behind its cleaning cocoon, restored to its former glory, with new paint and gilding, and then the Agency will turn its attention to the River Terrace, the view that many visitors admire from the embankment across the river. It was on Westminster Bridge, after all, that Wordsworth wrote,

> Earth has not anything to show more fair:
> Dull would he be of soul who could pass by
> A sight so touching in its majesty.

This washing of London's buildings has become worthwhile because of the decrease in pollution. Indeed, the amount of winter sunshine in central London is now the same as on the outskirts. (I can just hear someone saying, "That's not much to write home about.") The improvement has been achieved in part by the reduction of smoke from house chimneys since local authorities were empowered to declare smoke control zones within which only smokeless fuel could be burned and to help people pay for the installation of special grates for this purpose. Tighter statutes in manufacturing and maintenance, too, have ensured less smoke from trucks, buses, and other diesel-engined vehicles. Pollution from railway engines has been significantly cut by the switch from coal to electric and diesel power.

Britain's efforts in this field come under a Department of the Environment headed by Secretary of State Patrick Jenkin MP. There is also a Royal Commission on Environmental Pollution which was set up fifteen years ago to "advise on matters, both national and international, concerning the pollution of the environment; on the adequacy of research in this field; and the future possibility of danger to the environment."

Modestly, Patrick Jenkin, reviewing the past year, writes, "We in Britain are sometimes too modest about our achievements. This is certainly true in relation to the improvement of our environment. Indeed, to read our newspapers or watch our television, one might be tempted to believe that things are forever getting worse. In fact, the exact opposite is the case. Things are steadily getting better."

Mr. Jenkin does concede that some of the most worrying problems, such as acid rain, lie ahead on the international front. Britain will be spending more than $4 million in 1984/5 on research to help determine how acid deposition affects the environment. My impression is that if Britain addresses this problem with the enthusiasm evident in tackling problems on the home front, her European neighbors will have reason to be grateful.

February 28, 1985

Washing the Thames

LAST WEEK I spoke of successful efforts in Britain to come to grips with the pollution of the environment. Much, of course, still remains to be done. Some of Britain's estuaries, particularly those which are home to older industries and large populations, are grossly polluted and the cost of clean up will run into thousands of millions of pounds. But the example of what has been done with the London Thames is most encouraging.

Raphael Holinshed wrote in his *Chronicles* in 1578, "This noble river, the Thames, yields an infinite plenty of excellent sweet, and pleasant fish. . . . What should I say of the fat and sweet salmon daily taken in this stream, and in such plenty . . . that no river in Europe is able to exceed it." In the 1700's Joseph Addison said of a fellow countryman who described the Thames as the noblest river in Europe that this was one of the honest prejudices which naturally cleave to the heart of a true Englishman. The state of the Thames in succeeding years, however, would make even this honest prejudice hard to sustain. By 1830 salmon had completely disappeared. By 1920 the river was so polluted that marine life could not survive. By the mid 1970's the river was regarded as biologically dead, with an oxygen level of zero.

But . . . today the Thames has a 98% oxygen content, supports more than a hundred species of fish and attracts many varieties of birds. A seal has been spotted swimming past the House of Commons and salmon are there in quantity. A twenty year effort to roll back the tide of pollution has, according to Reuter news-agency, been called by ecology experts, the most successful campaign of its kind in the world.

There seem to have been two concerted assaults on the pollution of the Thames, in the mid-nineteenth century and now. The success of the current clean up is due in part to the measures taken earlier.

By the middle of the last century cholera and typhoid epidemics attributable at least in part to the river alarmed the authorities. Prince Albert, Queen Victoria's consort, was one who died. The problem was all too obvious to the inhabitants of London. 1856 was even known as the year of the big stink.

A year earlier Michael Faraday, the scientist, had written to *The Times* about a boat journey between Hungerford and London bridges: "The whole of the river was an opaque pale brown fluid. . . . Near the bridges the feculence rolled up in clouds so dense that they were visible at the surface." A member of parliament commented, "By perverse ingenuity one of the noblest of rivers has been changed into a cesspool." Parliament was finally spurred to action when a hot summer, according to one paper, created as much anxiety as the just occurred Indian mutiny. If the problem had been further away perhaps it would have taken even longer. But, as John Doxat writes in *The Living Thames,* "Sheets drenched in disinfectant had to be hung in the House of Commons in ineffective effort to dispel the prevailing stench."

The solution adopted was to create sewage bypasses on the north and south banks of the river. Into them would flow existing sewers and supplementary ones and then the sewage instead of emptying into the river in the heart of the city would be carried to a point ten miles away. The untreated sewage would be stored and then emptied into the river at the ebb tide so that it would be carried out to sea and dissolved by the waves. The quality of construction was such that many vital sewers built then are in operation today. The people ten miles down river were, of course, less satisfied by the solution. And it was a further decade before large scale and effective treatment of sewage was developed.

In 1880 London had a population of four and three quarter million. By 1939 the figure had nearly doubled. Also thirty years ago another man-made problem muddied the waters, so to speak. The use of detergents became then the prime cause of the river's deterioration. Between 1951 and 1961 the use of detergent increased threefold. There was the tragic case of a man who drowned because would-be rescuers could not see him through the foam. The new non-biodegradable detergents also decreased the efficiency of the sewage treatment plants by 30%.

Reading the accounts of how this disastrous situation was ended one is struck by the voluntary self-regulation of businesses who phased out non-biodegradable detergents and the fact that very few prosecutions have been needed against firms breaking environmental laws. One can salute, too, the vigor with which in the last ten years the Thames Water Authority has conducted a $280 million clean up project and monitors closely the river waters. The twelve million people who depend on the Thames can be grateful that, as Thames Water Authority spokesman Derek Gregg says, "It is now the cleanest industrial river in the world."

The poet Matthew Arnold once wrote,

> Oh, born in days when wits were fresh and clear,
> And life ran gaily on the sparkling Thames;
> Before this strange disease of modern life,
> With its sick hurry, its divided aims,
> Its heads o'ertaxed, its palsied hearts, was rife.

Well, the Thames has started to sparkle again. So perhaps, without lapsing into overconfidence about it, we should get on with tackling some of the other strange diseases of modern life.

February 21, 1985

8 Around the world

Costa Rica

IN FIVE YEARS' TIME this largely agricultural country will celebrate 100 years of democracy. It elects a new president every four
years. It abolished its armed forces 35 years ago and is so dedicated to peace that its most recent ex-president has worked to
establish a peace university. It has the highest literacy rate in
Latin America. It has been called the "Switzerland of Central
America." I am talking about Costa Rica.

Earlier this year we had a high-powered Costa Rican delegation in Portland. It included the country's vice president and its
minister for exports as well as legislators and businesspeople. It
was accompanied by the US ambassador and the head of the US
Agency for International Development. For Costa Rica wants to
expand its trade with Oregon which now totals seven million
dollars.

There are already a number of links between Costa Rica and
Oregon, some established for instance by Partners of the
Americas. These include the exchange of high school groups and
teachers and others in many professional and cultural fields.

Costa Rica has its problems. It is resisting pressures from the
United States to depart from its long-established neutrality and
militarize. It cannot entirely prevent its border airstrips from
being used by dissident Nicaraguans. It has to contend, like many
poorer countries, with high interest rates and fluctuating exchange rates and commodity prices. In the past five years it has
made huge strides in recovering from 100% inflation and a failure
to meet its international financial obligations. At the end of 1983
inflation was down to 11% and although the foreign debt was still
high, the country was up-to-date on interest payments. As the
visiting delegation made clear the country is also trying to overcome a negative balance in foreign trade.

In June Luis Alberto Monge, Costa Rica's President, addressed
the International Labor Organization in Geneva. Coming from a
trade union background and having himself worked with the ILO

he was warmly received. "We are a people without much economic, military or political influence," he said, "but our peaceful vocation, our dedication to freedom and our battle for social justice give us sufficient moral authority to tell the truth in these times of great world tension and in particular as concerns the dramatic situation of Central America. Costa Rica is a spiritual power because its people believe passionately in the strength of common sense, in the strength of determination, in the strength of moral values."

Last month, before addressing the ILO, President Monge visited the Moral Re-Armament conference center in Caux at the other end of the Lake of Geneva. He brought with him a party of 30 including five cabinet ministers. In April he had opened a Round Table conference for Moral Re-Armament in his capital city of San José.

It was through a visit to Caux he and three other Costa Ricans made 34 years ago that he had received, as he put it, "the sense of responsibility that led us to found the only political force that has taken the shape of a democratic political party." All four of them had subsequently become president.

Thanking the Swiss hosts at Caux, Monge said, "Many of the principles of Moral Re-Armament have been present in my spirit at the great turning points in my life." One of these principles which he said was vital in Central America where blood was being shed was that "we can only fight for peace if we have peace in ourselves and if we do all we can to pass it on to others." He announced that he would send Costa Ricans to the Caux session on the Americas and Europe in early August.

President Monge's recent trip through Europe has been in part an effort to counter what many Costa Ricans feel is disinformation being spread about their country's policies. He has succeeded in persuading the foreign ministers of the main EEC countries to meet this fall in San José to talk about Central America with Central Americans, with all the participants involved.

I got this news from the President's son, Guido, with whom I talked in Washington, DC last week. He works with the Inter-American Development Bank. As a democratic Central American Guido longs for America to take bolder steps to encourage reform and development in the area. He sees this as far more productive than the belief in a military resolution of the conflict. Support for the *contras* in Nicaragua, he says, not only undercuts sincere democrats in Central America but also becomes an excuse for the Nicaraguan government to depart from building a pluralistic society. If they had the choice, he puts it graphically, Costa Rica would like to pack its bags and leave the region. But it has to learn to live with its neighbors. "Costa Rica's only power," he told me, echoing his father's words, "is spiritual and moral power."

His father told the ILO, "We are vain enough to believe that the basic battle for Central America will take place in Costa Rica, and without arms. The spiritual strength of the people of Costa Rica will reinvigorate the atmosphere in the rest of Central America. We are called upon to demonstrate that our system of freedom is possible in our part of the world, that democracy works as a means of settling problems of production and to win battles in the struggle against underdevelopment and poverty. The freedom enjoyed by the people of Costa Rica must shine out as stars offering hope to the other neighboring people of Central America."

July 19, 1984

Disinvestment

I WANT TO TALK today about one of the most beautiful countries in the world, a country possessing some of the finest people of all races I have ever met, a country which could have a peaceful and prosperous future ahead of it, be a granary for food and a center for expertise for a whole continent and above all a demonstration to the world of how political, racial, and cultural differences can be a source not of division but of strength.

I am referring to South Africa, a country whose present terrible torment is splashed across our TV screens and newspaper headlines. I believe that any foreigner who wants to contribute to the debate about that country's future needs to have a vision for it as well as reactions to it.

We have looked at the sad events of the last days through the eyes of a white South African who is staying with us — an Afrikaner lady whose family settled there hundreds of years ago, who knows no other home, who has been working away peacefully, constructively, to break down the barriers between the races and who is as upset by the violence of the last days as any demonstrator outside any embassy.

Her presence with us underlines again for me the fact that issues in South Africa are not conveniently black and white. Indeed, the more I look at the situation the less I feel like saying, this or that is the right way of doing things.

Take the vexed issue of disinvestment. I don't want to take sides for or against it, only to say that one can with a good conscience support either policy. One can encourage continued participation in the life of South Africa in the belief that our presence there will give the best leverage for change; one can point to specific improvements which have been made thanks to policies which our companies have adopted; one can quote responsible black leaders in the country who tell us that disinvestment is anti-black and will harm most those it is intended to help; and that it will create a climate of confrontation rather than peaceful change.

On the other hand one can press for disinvestment in the belief that an honorable democracy like ours can have no truck with a racist minority government that tramples on the rights of blacks; that continued investment is only propping up a slave system; that some innocent people will have to suffer for the sake of progress; that all changes are cosmetic and do not touch the central issue of control.

I find myself in a dilemma when I look, for instance, at two statements which I believe to be true: 1) disinvestment seems likely to hurt the blacks most, and 2) the threat of disinvestment seems to speed the process of change on the part of whites. Such matters remind us in South Africa week that we should beware simplistic solutions.

The debate in South Africa is not, conversely, about the rights and wrongs of apartheid. Its deathknell has long since sounded, painful as the death throes will be. Apartheid has no future. It is discredited and simply doesn't work. The numbers of those who still believe in it are diminishing. The real debate within the country, a debate wrapped in fear, a fear which may have led to this week's tragic shootings, is how to replace apartheid without in the process destroying a great country for all its races.

The debate outside South Africa is equally not about whether we are for or against apartheid. It is not a public forum where we can display our righteousness to our peers. The system is clearly abhorrent to all but the most warped minds, not just to those with the shrillest voices. The real debate outside the country is about how we as foreigners can best help and not hinder the dismantling process.

On that score I read a perceptive article by the garden writer of *The Christian Science Monitor,* Peter Tonge, who happens to be a South African. He points out that the situation there is not simply one of true democracy versus racial exclusion. Within South Africa's borders there coexists an advanced Western society and the third world — pools of prosperity surrounded by sands of impoverishment. He believes that South African whites are having to face now what the whole Western world will have to face in the years to come in relation to the third world as a whole. That is, how to surrender what it believes it has earned for the sake of principle, or to put it in today's South African context, it is the rights of blacks to self-determination versus the rights of whites to keep what the West takes for granted.

"A solution to the South African situation that is equitable and relatively tranquil, and which does not shatter the economy," he writes, "may be as important to outsiders as it is to black and white South Africans. It might point the way for the rest of the world."

Tonge believes, too, that Pretoria will listen more readily to outside criticism if the tone is changed even if the substance is not. "Public comments on South Africa," he writes, "fairly drip with self-righteousness, which South Africans find more offensive than the criticism itself. Changing the tone won't be easy. It will require a better understanding of what it is like to be a minority white in that country."

Having a white South African staying with us helps us take that advice to heart.

March 28, 1985

Feeding India

THE FACT THAT INDIA is self-sufficient in food production is a remarkable and not widely known achievement. This does not mean that everyone is yet getting enough to eat. Some people do not have money to buy food. So there is no reason for complacency. But one can be grateful for a scale of progress in the direction of feeding people which would a few years ago have been thought impossible.

There are many imaginative schemes being developed in India, ranging from food for work programs to massive record-breaking irrigation projects. I'd like to tell you today about one hope-giving endeavor which has just come to my attention.

It is a new project which was described at a development "Dialogue" at Asia Plateau, Panchgani in January. It is being carried out in the South Indian state of Tamil Nadu and is called the Chief Minister's Nutritious Meal Program. This program is providing lunch for millions of children every day, has put 200,000 people to work and had been called a unique anti-poverty program which really reaches the poor and cannot be misused because one full meal is served at a time and is eaten on the spot.

By American standards it may not seem like a full meal but each needy preschool child gets 411 calories and each schoolchild 580 calories of food which they like and is good for them — sambar-rice, that is rice with pulses and vegetables.

The scheme was inaugurated last July simultaneously outside the towns through more than 50,000 rural feeding centers and two months later in urban areas through nearly 6000 centers. Now there are some 60,000 centers feeding on average 6.3 million children every day.

Announcing these results a senior official, Latika Padalkar, Additional Secretary of the Tamil Nadu Government, said, "Many of us who doubted have become firm believers. If there was a miracle, it was this, that the state machinery rose to the challenge, worked like a single person and made it possible to inaugurate the program in four short months."

Through nutrition, she said, the government was aiming at better health, reduced morbidity and mortality which in turn might encourage mothers to limit the size of their families. Fresh employment opportunities had been created for more than 100,000 rural women who work as cooks and helpers in the centers.

Preference was given to widows and destitute women, and women had been selected from the scheduled castes, the former untouchables. Women from higher castes not only send their children to these centers but also allow scheduled caste women to care for them. "It will take several decades before castes disappear," said Mrs. Padalkar. "However, we discern a trend towards harmony when, regardless of caste differences, all children sit together and share a common meal. Mothers are beginning to realize that these differences are man-made.

The cost per child works out at 45 paise, or five cents, per meal with a total of more than a billion rupees. "The State Government and more so the people of Tamil Nadu are determined to bear this burden," she said. People had already contributed voluntarily 20 million rupees. "They believe that investment in human resource development is investment in the future of the state and its own people."

It is interesting that the farm attached to the conference center at Asia Plateau is itself working on experiments which will help with the feeding of India. For fifteen years it has concentrated on developing new crops and methods appropriate for farmers in the surrounding villages. For instance, for the past two years it has been carrying out trials with Subabul. This remarkable leguminous tree, a native of Central America, is fast-growing and at elevations below 500 meters rapidly produces high yields of good quality wood both for firewood and commercial use.

At Asia Plateau where the elevation is around 1300 meters, Subabul has already proved to be an excellent fodder shrub. The foliage which is rich in protein is liked by the cattle and can be grown on poor soil or hillside land without fertilizer or irrigation, once the seedlings have been established. Even at Asia Plateau's height it produces considerable quantities of firewood.

At present approximately 6000 Subabul shrubs are growing on

the farm and it is hoped to increase the number by at least 10,000 next year. Some of the farm's cows have begun receiving Subabul foliage daily and the quality of concentrate being fed to these cows has been halved. The crossing of local breeds with pure-bred bulls is increasing in the villages but the farmers lack the protein-rich fodder needed for milk production; they cannot afford to buy expensive concentrated feed. The situation could be transformed if village farmers would grow Subabul on unproductive hill land.

Those working at Asia Plateau believe that once the value of Subabul is apparent, it will be widely grown to meet the needs of village farmers, many of whom only cultivate small plots of land and have no irrigation.

John Porteous, a New Zealander who left his own farm to come and work unpaid at Asia Plateau and who died last year, said, "Agriculture must ensure that every man, woman and child on earth is adequately nourished in body, mind and spirit. It is towards this giant task that we at Asia Plateau have dedicated our lives. India can be fed. Her supple hands, soiled with the dignity of labor, will provide an abundance of food and wealth for mankind."

March 3, 1983

Royalty

AMERICANS seem to have a sort of love-hate relationship with royalty. That Princess Diana is expecting a baby in September gets far more column inches than many a more important story. Despite old George III, millions of Americans were glued to their TV screens at Prince Charles and Lady Diana's wedding, and I saw several ladies around Portland who were trying to look like the princess. When Britain's royalty visits these shores, Britain's official representatives are inundated with requests to meet them.

Americans may feel uncomfortable with the concept of royalty. They may even refuse to curtsy or bow to mere mortals or accord them titles like "your majesty" or "your royal highness" or resent the idea of treating anyone else with special dignity. In fact, I happened to be at a royal wedding recently. When a photographer appeared, one guest, by chance an Oregonian, took the king's arm and posed with him. I do not think the king was amused.

We have our pseudo-royalty in this country, our princesses and their courts, not to mention Hollywood. We have our own Portland Royal Rosarians and my wife keeps reminding me that they, too, need to be treated with due respect. I suppose that as we in Britain have our own royalty I tend not to take seriously anything other than, as the Coca-Cola slogan goes, the real thing.

It may be hard for some people here to grasp the affection and respect with which our royal family are regarded in Britain. It is not just the institution. For nearly fifty years the members of our royal family have contributed to the cohesion of our national life by the example they set of Christian family life, of sound values and healthy attitudes, of service. Some of the royal family may get a bit irritated with the press. Buckingham Palace has twice recently appealed to the press to respect the privacy of the royal family on vacation. But considering the distortions they sometimes have to put up with, the royal family are pretty long-suffering.

Jean Marcilly, former Editor in Chief of *France Dimanche,* made a study of the way the British royal family was treated by the French press between 1958 and 1972. During that period the French popular press reported 63 times that the Queen had abdicated, 73 times that she had been on the point of breakup with Prince Philip. The papers said that she had been "fed up" 112 times, on the verge of nervous breakdown 32 times, had 43 unhappy nights and 27 nightmares. Her life had been threatened 29 times and she was also supposed to have expelled Lord Snowdon from court 151 times.

Naturally the British press does not go as far off track as that. They would undermine their credibility. Michael Shea, the Queen's Press Secretary, told *The Christian Science Monitor* earlier this month, "There are very few nasty stories in the British press. There is no war between Fleet Street and the Palace." He reports that the criticism of Princess Anne and Princess Margaret has gone, particularly since Princess Anne went to Africa for the

Save the Children Fund. Prince Andrew, he says, gets a fantastic and supportive mail.

It is estimated that the royal family will cost Britain about 35 million dollars this year. This is a 4% increase which, according to *The Guardian* is "to prevent a threatened deterioration in the majesty of Britain's greatest tourist attraction."

Members of the royal family have made some memorable speeches in recent years. Prince Charles has given challenging talks on freedom, stressing what we can learn from those who have lost it. He told the London Press Club to which I belong, "Our protection depends on the mystical power which from time immemorial has been called God and whose relationship to man seems to depend on man's relationship to his inner voice. It also depends on a free press which is constantly aware of its vital, responsible and extraordinarily powerful voice."

In a speech at Alberta University last year he spoke of what was owed to those who deep down have high expectations of people like him. "We have," he said, "an increasing obligation to concentrate on developing our moral courage and a corresponding awareness of that inner force that we all possess, but without which we will be unable to resist that shadow of authoritarianism and at the same time provide a beam of hope, like a lighthouse on a stormy cliff top, for those who suffer in silence."

Each year Queen Elizabeth makes a Christmas broadcast to Britain and the Commonwealth. This year she said, "The greatest problem in the world today remains the gap between rich and poor countries, and we shall not begin to close the gap until we hear less about nationalism and more about interdependence." The Queen came under attack from some who claimed that she had more sympathy with immigrants and foreigners than with "her own people." But, as Patrick Keatley wrote in *The Guardian*, "Perhaps the real crime of the Queen in the eyes of her new critics is that she is unrepentantly non-racial."

I would add just one point. Many people get flustered by titles. I was at an international conference. A British worker was speaking. The American ambassador walked in. The worker knew it was someone important; he didn't want to demote him. He stammered, "Welcome, your majesty."

March 1, 1984

United nations

THE UNITED NATIONS, judging by recent newspaper articles is in need of support and change. A UPI story this week in *The Oregonian* says that the United Nations is anything but united. Its two main bodies—the General Assembly and the Security Council — are roundly disrespected and universally ignored. Critics, the news story continues, say the United Nations is "nothing more than a carnival of slick jugglers and self-serving sideshow men who come to New York City to eat in posh restaurants, illegally park their limousines and shamelessly chase tall blonds." The article continues in the same vein. And as the reporter is talking about some of my friends who, I happen to know, have a great deal of idealism and work very hard, I think a word of support for the United Nations from me in United Nations week would not be out of place.

It is true that in recent crises the UN General Assembly and Security Council have been found wanting, and even its new Secretary General has some strong criticisms. But I'd like to set against that UPI article what a *New York Times* correspondent wrote last month under the headline "As the assembly speakers drone, an unsung staff makes UN hum." The correspondent wrote, "Today, while foreign ministers from the capitals of the world discussed the Middle East, Latin America, South Africa and the international economic crisis, the permanent staff of the Secretariat wrestled with more mundane but, to tens of millions of people, more immediate issues.

"For example, the Secretariat announced that three more countries had ratified the convention on the elimination of all forms of discrimination against women. So far 42 countries have ratified or acceded to the convention. While the speakers in the General Assembly refer in general terms to the worldwide erosion of human rights, the chairman of the United Nations Anti-Apartheid Committee zeroed in on the Government of South Africa and accused it of increasing repression against non-whites. While General Assembly speakers were talking in vague terms today about increasing problems in the third world, the Secretariat issued a statement from the Director General of the United

Nations Food and Agriculture Organization . . . that 40% of the organization's 1982-3 budget of $368 million would be 'of direct and exclusive benefit to Africa' and that FAO was presently carrying out 580 field projects on that continent. Again, while foreign ministers were warning of worsening economic conditions in the third world, the Secretariat announced some $93.4 million in World Bank and International Development Association loans to seven countries for such projects as a kraft paper mill, farm credit and agricultural policy planning." And one could add, of course, to that list the work of the United Nations Childrens' Fund.

Of course, it is the political tip of the iceberg, the General Assembly, that tends to draw the headlines and I'd like to take you back for a moment to a little-remembered event from which we could draw encouragement. It was August 1958. The Middle East was in uproar. US marines had been flown into Lebanon. The Russians were moving armor south to reinforce Syria. By the 20th *The Times* of London was calling it "the most urgent and baffling problem in the world" and saying that any possibility of a settlement had disappeared. Yet the next day it could run the headline "Arab states find peace formula" and the next day "Unanimous vote for Arab plan." "Overnight," the paper said, "an almost magical transformation came over the scene where until yesterday the General Assembly . . . could not see how to extricate itself from the mire." The paper's editorial said that the resolution was courteously phrased and there was no hint of condemnation. Even Israel had voted favorably.

How did this happen? Much of it goes back to one man who had no official position at the UN, Abdul Khalek Hassouna, Secretary General of the Arab League. Here was a man whom I incidentally met at the Moral Re-Armament conference center in Switzerland who was accustomed to following the thoughts that came to him in a time of quiet to listen for guidance from God. These thoughts had propelled him to New York, inspired him to get together the representatives of the ten Arab nations, and to work to bridge the gulf between the two main groupings of Arab opinion. He sought, he says, to raise the discussions above claims and counterclaims and move from who is right to what is right.

Finally a resolution was agreed on. Because the Arabs were united everyone else supported it. Dag Hammarskjold called the resolution one of the strongest ever adopted by the UN. The *Washington Post* called it "a triumph for Hassouna." Hassouna himself told a fellow journalist, "As I returned to my room that night I could think of nothing, do nothing, but thank God."

I guess what we need at the UN as well possibly as structural reorganization is just more peacemakers like Hassouna.

October 14, 1982

On an Indian train

MANY OF US will have read, at a safe distance, of the bloodletting in India after the assassination of Mrs. Gandhi. I learned this week of the experiences of a friend of mine which bring home the awful reality of those hours. They underline the amazing power of recovery of the human body and the amazing power of forgiveness in the human spirit.

Sushobha Barve, a Hindu dietician who is responsible for the kitchens at the Moral Re-Armament conference center at Asia Plateau, Panchgani, India, was travelling in a train with a friend when the news broke of Mrs. Gandhi's murder by Sikhs. In their compartment were two Sikh businessmen.

At first, she reports, there was an almost unnaturally peaceful feel about the continuing train journey. Fellow passengers discounted the fears of the Sikhs. But as the hours ticked by the train began stopping. There was rumor that a Sikh had been pulled off the train and shaved, an affront to his faith. Sushobha was concerned how to protect the Sikhs. She moved from the window to the door. They moved to the top bunks.

In one town a gang of villagers entered the compartment but she managed to talk them out of mischief. At the next stop, however, the train was surrounded by villagers armed with sticks. Three times their compartment was searched. The fourth time the intruders wanted to know who was in the top bunk. They pulled off the sheet and discovered the two men. Sushobha tried to shield them and was seized. One man held her neck and hand. She was asked if she was travelling with the Sikhs. She said she was from Maharashtra, but her costume was from the Punjab, the Sikh homeland. She was wearing a silver bangle, but her assailant thought at first it was the steel bangle of a Sikh. "How dare you assault a woman," she said. He let go and wouldn't look her in the face. The Sikh men were pulled out, beaten until they seemed dead, and thrown back into the compartment. Then everything was looted. The train started again. It was discovered that the men were not dead. At the next stop the two ladies could only watch helplessly as the bodies were thrown off, stoned and then set on fire. They had been the only ones who tried to prevent what happened.

Thinking about the events shortly afterwards Sushobha said that she never dreamt that her generation would ever witness killings comparable to the period after partition, a period dramatized for us in the West through the *Gandhi* film. "It was gruesome," she wrote to a friend. "But even when the villager held me by the neck I felt comforted by God's love and protection. God gave me the right words to say which at least convinced one man. But," she asked, "what was God's purpose in allowing us to go through this? How are we going to repent and cleanse our sins? Is it possible to heal wounds between Hindus and Sikhs?"

A month later she was still feeling anger and guilt about those hours on the train. "I was tortured at night by the thought of not being able to save the lives of the two innocent men." She decided to accept the responsibility for what Hindus had done. "It was a painful process," she remembers, "but once accepted I was shown the steps I should take." She felt that she should write letters to Sikhs, some known by her, some not. As a Hindu, she wrote, she wanted to apologize unconditionally for what her people had done. She asked forgiveness. Khushwant Singh, a well known writer and Sikh spokesman, replied in a handwritten note, "I was in tears as I read your letter. As long as we have people like you around we will survive as a nation."

It was one thing to write letters of that kind, already a difficult step. It was another to visit Sikhs. This Sushobha also decided to do. She went to see a Sikh couple whose factories had been

burned down. Again she made an unconditional apology for the
deep wounds and humiliation. Husband and wife were in tears.
Usha, the wife, held her hand. "To hear what you have just said,"
she told Sushobha, "makes me feel that all we have gone through
during the last two months was worth it and is healed."

But still Sushobha could not keep out her mind the image of the
train victims. She tried unsuccessfully to get information about
them. Then came word that indicated one of them was alive. She
had an impelling sense that she must travel the 1200 miles to
where they came from. She had not been open to it earlier but
knew that she would not have peace of heart until she had done
so. She was fearful how a Hindu would be received.

"I cannot express the joy I felt when I saw Bupendra Singh
lying in his bed," she writes. "I was not greeted with hostility but
with courtesy, not formally but as an old friend of the family."
The room soon filled with family members and as the story was
pieced together all felt that God had heard their prayers and not
let them down. "It was a chain of miracles," believes Sushobha.
She even discovered that the other passenger, Govinder, had also
survived.

As Bupendra had lain on the ground pretending to be unconscious he had somehow managed to turn on his side and extin-
guish the fire. Govinder, who had been unconscious, was
awakened by his skin burning. He, too, managed to get out of his
burning clothes. In what seemed to them minutes a group of
police arrived and did their best to save them — this at a time
when most police were inactive. The Sikhs remember that as they
were carried, their bearers chanted *mantras,* prayers, for the
dead. They were so badly burned that friends at the hospital
didn't recognize them. Besides body burns, Govinder needed 152
stitches in his head. The doctor told the family, "Why have you
brought me a dead body?" "It was a medical challenge," said
Bupendra. "They struggled for two and a half months to put life
back into him and he has just returned home."

Sushobha expressed sorrow at not being able to protect them.
"We feel bad that you had to suffer because of us," responded
Bupendra. "We remember your arguing with those men and saw
the first *lathi,* stick, hit you. The men who took us talked of

finding the women who were with us and we were worried. We had not known what had become of you."

"Bupendra and his family were free of bitterness at a time when they had every reason to be bitter," reports Sushobha. "Even the most inhuman suffering had not killed the fine human qualities of courage, compassion, vision of the future, and gratitude to all who had helped them, us, policemen, doctors, God for the gift of new life."

At the recent Dialogue on Development at Asia Plateau, Sushobha said, "Reconciliation and reconstruction of human lives and relationships is going to be a painful process. But the essential is men and women who are willing and dare to break the chain of hate and revenge."

February 28, 1985

New Japan

JAPAN has a new Prime Minister, Yashuhiro Nakasone. I remember meeting him thirty two years ago when he was the youngest member of the Diet, the Japanese Parliament, and part of a Japanese delegation of 76 who came to the Moral Re-Armament conference center in Caux, Switzerland. The delegation, which included the mayors of Hiroshima and Nagasaki, was the first such large group of senior Japanese to travel to the West after World War II. Before they left, Prime Minister Shigeru Yoshida told them, "In 1870 a representative group of Japanese travelled to the West. On their return they changed the course of Japanese life. I believe that when this delegation returns, you, too, will open a new page in our history."

This has indeed happened according to some Japanese who now say that their astounding economic progress is linked with the application of the ideas they learned on that historic trip.

On their way home in 1950 the Japanese delegation was received in Washington, DC. Less than five years after the cessation of hostilities one of them, a Member of Parliament, Chojiro Kuriyama, spoke on the floor of the Senate and said, "We are sincerely sorry for Japan's big mistake. We broke almost a century-old friendship between our two countries."

The *Saturday Evening Post* commented editorially, "Mr. Kuriyama's statement would be hard for an American to understand . . . the idea of a nation admitting that it could be mistaken has a refreshing impact. . . . Perhaps even Americans could think up a few past occasions of which it could safely be said, 'We certainly fouled up things that time.' " *The New York Times* commented, "For a moment one could see out of the present darkness into the years when all men may be brothers."

Minority leader Joseph Martin, joining Vice-President Barkley and Speaker Sam Rayburn and others in welcoming the Japanese, said, "We want to make Japan one of the great countries of the world, a country that will join with us and the other forces that will fight for freedom and for better days for people everywhere. The peoples of our two great countries working together can be a positive force for better things for all the people of the world."

Today that still applies.

Thanks to far-seeing US policies, thanks to influences like those which so deeply affected those 76 Japanese as they travelled across the world, thanks above all to the energies and imagination of their own people Japan today is a nation which is looked to as an example in many areas, particularly industry.

In recent years Japanese have played a prominent part in the industrial conferences which have taken place each summer in Caux where the earlier group came just after the war. This past summer was no exception and I have this week received a printed report of the 1982 industrial session there. Its theme was "World industry — confrontation or a common task?" It dealt with the questions: Can industry build bridges between nations and contribute to peace? Can people everywhere have work and fulfillment? Can industry develop the best qualities in people?

The report quotes Nobutane Kiuchi, President of the Japanese Institute of World Economy, "We must return to fundamentals. Mass production was needed to answer poverty. But once poverty is removed, it loses its point so that the means can become an end in itself. We need to reconsider our aims."

But one of the most interesting comments relating to Japan

came from an American, Stephen Fuller, a former Vice-President of General Motors and now a professor at the Harvard Business School. He said that in a recent article a prominent Japanese management consultant had given a list of the priorities of various relationships within the Japanese business community. In order of importance the priorities were: 1) employees, 2) suppliers, 3) customers, 4) the local communities in which the firm operates, 5) the national government, 6) bankers, and 7) stockholders.

"I suggest," said Professor Fuller, "if the priorities of Japanese business were totally reversed that one would approximate the traditional priorities of most Western business enterprises. It seems to me," he said, "that we have to thank the intense competition that many of our basic industries face, for example, from Japan, because without that pressure we might not look at the way we manage people."

Human resource management in many US organizations, he said, left much to be desired. Our record of poor quality, sluggish productivity and uninvolved employees proved it. "Today," he told the conference, "worldwide competition requires courageous innovations in management style and techniques. But our human resources will not be better managed until we change our priorities. They will not be better managed until we adopt managerial philosophies that rest on faith in people, that place people ahead of profits."

The Japanese, as can be seen from that management consultant's list, are putting priority on people. Delegations from the West are now travelling to Japan to learn from them. Next May Japan will be hosting a major Moral Re-Armament industrial conference. As the then Japanese Foreign Minister, Yoshio Sakuranchi, told the Budget Committee of the Japanese House of Representatives earlier this year, such Moral Re-Armament conferences provide "valuable opportunities for one to exchange information and develop international understanding."

December 16, 1982

9 Personalities

The Dalai Lama

MY WIFE AND I had the chance a few days ago to pay our respects
to one of the great spiritual leaders of our time—the Dalai Lama.
We had met him before, I in London some years back and my
wife in Dharmsala shortly after he had to flee from the Chinese
repression in Tibet and make his home in that Indian village in the
Himalayan foothills.

We were glad to find him relaxed despite an arduous six weeks
in the United States where he met and conferred with many
individuals and groups. His spirit seemed buoyant and not
weighed down by the sufferings of his people and his more than
25 years in exile. He was outgoing to all who approached him.
Though he did admit to a little homesickness for India.

His Holiness was in the area to meet members of the Oregon
and Washington Tibetan community.

At Portland airport some 200 people were on hand to greet the
49-year-old monk who is regarded as the most respected Buddhist
figure in the world. "He is like the Pope to us," an older Vietnamese, an accountant with the city of Portland, explained to me.
Security was unobtrusive but tight. In fact, I inadvertently
alarmed a policewoman as I whipped out my notebook when the
Dalai Lama paused to answer the questions of a TV reporter. The
welcome was warm as the maroon-robed monk walked along
between a corridor of well-wishers, at his side an elderly local
retired businessman, Stanley Bishoprick, known affectionately by
members of the Portland Tibetan community as "granddaddy"
because of his concern over the years for their work and welfare.
I stood with Tibetans who had been here for many years and also
members, white and black, of the small Portland Buddhist center.
A beautiful maroon Lincoln Continental that matched the Dalai
Lama's robes was waiting to whisk the Tibetan leader away to
Seaside where he was to spend two nights. The reception had

been a little low key, one Tibetan informed me, lest they be confused with the Rajneeshis.

At Seaside the Dalai Lama spoke to the Tibetan community, friends, and the press. I found myself between a charming petite Buddhist nun from Seattle who was of course delighted to have a personal word from her spiritual mentor and an experienced American foreign correspondent who was equally delighted in his own way to get on tape some answers from the head of the Tibetan government in exile.

After a welcome from the Tibetan community, from the Mayor of Seaside, and on behalf of Governor Atiyeh — during which formal proceedings the visiting dignitary seemed to be examining the ceiling with amused detachment—he then spoke to us.

Turning to his own people he expressed gratitude for what they had gained from their ten or fifteen years in the area and also for the way they had preserved their identity and culture. To the wider audience he stressed the need for the coming together of the world community. He was a Tibetan, he said, a Buddhist, a monk, from what some people called Shangri-la, a country with a small population, a large area, materially poor, spiritually rich. Here was he among friends with a quite different culture and circumstances. But these were superficial differences. We were all the same human beings, with the same blood, the same flesh. Some had noses that were bigger than others, he added lightly. Some had a different color. But the human hearts are the same, he went on, with the same feelings and desires. In that sense the more than 4 billion people on earth are brothers and sisters. That kind of basic teaching is needed, he told his audience. It wasn't even a question of Holy teaching but a matter of survival and development.

In some ways what the Buddhist leader said was simple, was commonsense, almost naive. If it had come from somebody else. But here was a man who from an early age had known the reality and pain of invading armies, of Communist ideology, of loss of homeland.

The Dalai Lama touched on this loss of his own country through no misbehavior of its own people. And although he didn't spell it out, one was reminded of the Chinese rape of this mountain land, of the killing of over a million of its people, of the destruction of 95% of the ancient temples and monasteries, and of the imprisonment of a quarter of a million more Tibetans during the Cultural revolution. And one knew that much as he longed to visit his country again, his own people there had advised against it because of danger to his life.

After all he has been through one could expect to find a man consumed by bitterness or living in the past. Yet there is no trace of this. Indeed, quite the opposite.

I remember the Dalai Lama's stimulating assertion at the conference in Caux, Switzerland, last summer. Tolerance and forgiveness were the key methods of minimizing hatred, he said, and you could learn these things from your enemy. You could not feel hatred, disrespect or anger towards your *guru* (teacher) so you could not learn tolerance, forgiveness and patience from him, or from your best friend. Hatred usually arose from your enemy. When you met him, that was the golden opportunity to test how much you practiced what you believed. If we thought along these lines, he said, we might feel gratitude towards our enemy.

The Dalai Lama's generous approach is a challenge to all of us.

November 1, 1984

William Wilberforce

IT MAY SEEM a bit of a paradox that in Black History month I should talk about a great white man. But the connection will soon become clear. I want to tell you about a politician who in his time became known as the conscience of England. His name is William Wilberforce and he lived in the 18th century, a time of much cruelty and corruption, perhaps typified by the heartlessness of the slave trade, one of the country's most profitable industries and described this week by Ron Herndon, Co-Chairman of the Black United Front, as "one of the most horrible chapters ever written in history."

Wilberforce was well off, had great charm, and just 200 years ago, at the age of 21, entered the British Parliament. Three years later his closest friend became prime minister and he had the world at his feet. But a remarkable change came into his life. He could have become prime minister himself, one historian believes, if he had preferred party to mankind, but instead he was set on a different course of service.

He faced the fact that he had really achieved nothing worthwhile in his first years in Parliament, for, as he said, "My own distinction was my darling object." He accepted a larger commission. "God Almighty has laid before me two great objects," he wrote in his diary, "the abolition of the slave trade and the reformation of manners," which we might call the whole moral climate of the country.

Wilberforce decided to put these new objects before claims of political party, before possibility of preferment, before popularity. He began what became for him a lifelong habit of rising early to spend time in meditation. He enlisted around him a team of men in public life that was said to be more talented than the cabinet. Indeed, they would meet in what they called "cabinet councils," where they devised an imaginative strategy to advance their twin aims privately and publicly. They were nicknamed "the saints."

Wilberforce became one of the best-loved men in England but also one of the most hated. His life was threatened by West Indian sea captains, he was opposed by the Establishment, cold-shouldered by royalty, and endured all sorts of attempts at character assassination. He was never a strong man, nor a well man. John Wesley, the founder of Methodism, in the very last letter he ever wrote, cautioned Wilberforce, "Unless God has raised you for this very thing, you will be worn out by the opposition of men and devils, but if God is with you who can be against you?"

Wilberforce kept at it—for forty-six years. After twenty years of unrelenting battle the House of Commons passed the bill abolishing the slave trade by 283 votes to 16. "Well, Henry," Wilberforce said to his colleague Thornton that evening, "what shall we abolish next?" Twenty-six years later, on his deathbed, Wilberforce was given the news that within a year all 800,000 slaves in British territories were to be set free.

Meanwhile such a change of moral climate, the second great object, had occurred that it was reckoned scarcely a hundred leading families remained where at least one member had not undergone what was called the "great change," and the groundwork was laid for many important reforms and democratic developments that followed.

Wilberforce's achievements are important to remember for they show that it is not economic pressures alone which dictate policy. Modern research has made it clear that the slave trade was actually abolished when it was at its most profitable. Wilberforce's life shows that individuals are not helpless before events when they decide to put a great aim ahead of their own comfort and ambition, and, perhaps just as important, know how, as Wilberforce did, to enlist and work with others for that aim. Wilberforce's biographer, John Pollock, makes the point, "Wilberforce proved that one man can change his times, but he cannot do it alone."

February 4, 1982

Saidie Patterson

SAIDIE PATTERSON, one of the great women of Ireland, a staunch Methodist and fighter for Moral Re-Armament and a friend of our family for 35 years, has just died. When I interviewed Irish Nobel Peace Prize winner Betty Williams and asked her if she knew Saidie Patterson, she responded, "You mean 'our Saidie.' " For Saidie was regarded as the mother of the women's peace movement in Northern Ireland. As Chairman of the Women Together movement she led a march of 50,000 women through the Protestant and Catholic areas of the city. Saidie, a Protestant, said on that occasion, "The last time I walked up the Shankhill, the Catholic area, with Catholics was in the early '30s when we were marching to the workhouse for bread and some of us were in our bare feet. Today we walked up the Shankhill not as Protestants or Catholics but as children of the King of Kings."

She was referring to her lifelong battle for the women textile workers. Born in a working class family in Belfast in 1906 in a house she lived in all her life, Saidie had to go to work in the local linen mills at the age of 12 when her mother died and she was left to look after her sick father and six brothers and sisters. She helped organize the women textile workers and led some of their historic strikes, became the first woman official in the Transport and General Workers Union and later the first woman chairman of the Northern Ireland Labour Party.

Receiving an honorary degree in 1977 she reminded her audience what life was like in those early days when textiles was one of the main industries employing 100,000, mostly women. "We were plentiful and cheap," she said. "The working week was one of 55 hours and many a time we worked 60; and no overtime was paid. A holiday was regarded as a lay-off without pay." Women, she told the university audience, worked until 6 at night, babies were often born perhaps two hours later the same evening and the women had to be back at work within 48 hours or lose their jobs. Children of 11 went three days to school and three to work. "We who produced the finest linen in the world had to be content with the newspapers on our tables, too poor to buy what we produced. Often we slept on sheets made from flour bags."

Out of such injustice a passion was born in Saidie which was never extinguished. A visit to the Moral Re-Armament conference center in Switzerland, however, transformed her militant but bitter fight for the workers into an all-embracing commitment to bridge the differences between all people and answer hatred everywhere.

For her subsequent work to bring Catholics and Protestants together she was given five international awards. But she was also attacked. During one rally, when she was already in her seventies, she was beaten up but saved by Catholic women. She was in hospital for months with an injured spine, but all the time enlisting, as she put it, converts for the cause. "Isn't it amazing," she observed, "how Protestants and Catholics share one another's blood on the transfusion table." She wrote me from hospital, "My daily experience is that the Holy Spirit is uniting humanity through men and women who listen and obey. I believe Ireland will be used to take God's answer to the world."

When Saidie was given the first World Methodist Peace Award, the citation stated, "She has sat with the men of violence and dissuaded them from bombing and shooting." At the very moment the TV cameras were filming her reaction to the award the news came in that her great-nephew had been gunned down in an IRA ambush. "The news made my blood run cold," she said, "but I prayed that bitterness would not enter my heart. I was more determined than ever to continue the work for peace." Later that night she said on television, "Young man, you who killed some-one dear to me today have done a terrible thing. But there is no bitterness, only sadness in my heart. Nor do I want anyone in Northern Ireland to react with bitterness. We have enough of that."

When the Pope visited Ireland, Saidie was one of those who helped collect half a million Protestant signatures urging him to visit the North. When she took the signatures to the Papal Nuncio she was invited to speak at the International Vigil for Peace and Reconciliation to be held in the Pope's honor in Dublin's St. Patrick's Cathedral. She said at the Vigil, "Which one of you here tonight picked your parents? Why then do we battle about our origins?" Describing the occasion later, she said, "I had a long talk with the Good Lord. He told me what to say. I started by asking if everybody there that night were arrested for being a Christian, would there be enough evidence to convict you and me. I told them it was one thing to pray during a crisis but it is another thing so to live that it does not happen again." She received 800 letters after her address.

Even in her late seventies, crippled with arthritis, hampered by her injuries, and walking on crutches, she would be out touring the countryside, attending four or five meetings a week, particu-larly with young people. "I'm all right from the neck up," she would joke. Indeed, her pithy remarks, Saidieisms as they were called, were her trademark. To the male trade unionists she would say, "If the men would pass more pubs and fewer resolutions we'd be a good deal better off." One of her last pieces of advice, on bigotry, "Leave it aside. It went out with hobble skirts and button boots."

Mother Teresa of Calcutta said that Saidie had kept her vows of poverty, chastity and obedience as irrevocably as any nun. David Bleakley, a former cabinet minister in Northern Ireland and Saidie's biographer, said at her funeral, "An Ireland full of Saidie Patterson's would be an island at peace."

March 7, 1985

Prime Minister Hawke

THEY SAY that the difference between an Australian and an Englishman is this. An Englishman walks into a hotel as if he owns the place. An Australian walks in looking as if he doesn't give a damn who owns it. Certainly there is a rugged individualism in Australia, a strength of will and character which has become increasingly known to Americans through Australian films. Her new Prime Minister, Bob Hawke, is no exception to that tough, bluff image. Hearing him speak to the National Press Club in Washington, as I did recently, one realized that one was listening to a man to be reckoned with on the world scene.

On assuming office last March he immediately launched what has been described as the most important conference in Australia since World War II. It was a continuation of a consistent theme of his ten year's presidency of Australia's trade unions, that is getting people to end confrontation and conflict and work together. We might learn from what he is attempting in Australia.

Broadcast live over television and radio, the five-day conference drew a hundred top politicians, union bosses, captains of industry and leaders of farming organizations who addressed the urgent economic questions facing the country. Each delegate received a 300 page document of statistics outlining the seriousness of a situation which includes an estimated $8500 million budget deficit for 1983-84.

The conference, while having no decision-making powers, produced broadly acceptable guidelines for economic policy, with an unexpected degree of give and take on the part of representatives of management and labor. Writing in *The Industrial Pioneer* one commentator said, "What Australia witnessed is tantamount to statesmanship. It is the spirit of a government which sincerely believes that policies, however right and necessary, may not be worth the paper they are written on unless the major parties most affected find mutual agreement in their formulation."

Recently I received from Australia a rather unusual page torn from a newspaper. It was a full-page advertisement taken out by the government as a follow-up to this conference. Two-thirds of the page is black with the words superimposed in white, "The next summit. Fifteen million people are invited." The text alongside reads, "The first Economic Summit in Canberra brought together 100 leaders of various groups in our community. It set the directions that Australia will take in the future. Agreement was reached on how to tackle a range of serious problems. Such as creating jobs, boosting the housing industry, and creating a prices and incomes policy that is fair to everyone. It was an important event. However the next Summit is the big one. Its aim is to turn all of the talking into action. The next Summit is not an event. It is an attitude. A state of mind. Every Australian must come to realize that we're all in this together. The severe economic problems that face our country are *our* problems. If they are to be fixed, then we *all* must play our part in fixing them. It will mean an attitude of co-operation, of working together. It may mean certain sacrifices. But so long as the sacrifices are shared fairly, it will be for the good of all Australians. Very soon the government will announce the first of its economic plans, stemming from the Canberra Summit. On that day every Australian will be shown how they can contribute to Australia's economic recovery. With your co-operation, the next Summit will start that day."

Prime Minister Hawke's swift rise to power—he only entered Parliament three years ago—comes at a time when many Australians have grown weary of divisive political bickering and are eager for a non-partisan attack on increasing unemployment and inflation.

After returning from a Rhodes Scholarship at Oxford, Hawke worked steadily through the trade union movement to a position of high profile and popularity in the country. Although evoking a certain distrust in some quarters because of his union background and supposed demagoguery, he has always proclaimed consensus as the cornerstone of his approach. Indeed, he faces more opposition from the left of his own party than from the opposition benches in Parliament. Last month he won strong support from his own party in Parliament. *The Australian* called it "a day of victory over Labor's left wing."

Over the years as an Australian representative at the ILO in Geneva — he was eight years on its governing body — he established friendships with world leaders which stand him now in good stead. His administration has been stepping up successive governments' policies of being more involved in Asia, with overtures to Indonesia, Japan, Vietnam and China. Coming straight from Peking to Washington, he offered President Reagan to be a medium to secure better relations between the US and China. At the National Press Club he stressed the need to go beyond Benjamin Franklin to a declaration of interdependence. However unpalatable it might be, he said, we had to recognize that interdependence was global and universal. On the Soviet Union, he said it was better to engage in dialogue rather than attempt to isolate it.

Only two nations, Australia and New Zealand, have fought alongside American troops in four wars — World Wars I and II, Korea and Vietnam. And Hawke assured Reagan whom he invited to Australia that his country would remain America's most constructive ally. "It has been a great relationship in peace and war," he said.

In an interview with Australia's *Women's Weekly* four years ago, he explained his popularity, "The Australians, basically, are a gregarious, friendly mob. They see a fellow who's not stuck up, he's one of them — I don't think I give myself any airs — and they feel it's legitimate for them to trust me as a mate."

He also said about politics, "We've got to talk about the issues. We've got to recognize that we haven't got a monopoly on wisdom and that the other bloke hasn't got a monopoly on stupidity."

It looks as if the new prime minister might give new meaning to the word hawk.

August 11, 1983

Pauli Snellman

AT THE AGE OF 14 Pauli Snellman stood alone, armed with only a
rifle, guarding a railway bridge against the Russians. It was the
Winter War of 1940 when Finland was resisting a Russian invasion. Dressed in an army greatcoat several sizes too large, with
toes frozen in minus 40 degrees temperature, he was two hours
on, four hours off, night and day, with two kilometers to ski to
camp. The Finns were up against a population forty times theirs.
"It was a humanly hopeless case," Snellman remembers, "but the
people fought and rather miraculously our freedom was saved."

A great grandson of a founder of modern Finland, Snellman is
one of the people I met this summer at the Moral Re-Armament
conference in Caux, Switzerland.

Today the tall, distinguished-looking Finn is Chief Inspector in
the Ministry of Labor, representing his country at international
conferences. He has not lost his passion for freedom, nor, he
maintains, have his fellow countrymen and women. Finland has,
he points out, a reserve of 700,000 troops. But, bordering as they
do on the Soviet Union, they have had to exercise wisdom and
restraint in public policies. "Our geography is our fate," he told
me. "We are where in time of crisis no Western country can ever
really help us."

Freedom from fear was the element that stood out in our conversation at Caux. "It is immensely important to overcome fear,"
he stressed. "Fear clogs up creative thinking and openness to new
perspectives. It makes some people too preoccupied by what the
Communists are doing and turns others into wishful thinkers who
want to believe there are no threats." He was still tempted in both
directions and had to overcome fear every day. But he is helped
by a decision he made when he first joined the Labor Ministry.

Not wanting to be dominated by the bureaucracy, the Finnish
civil servant had decided, even as a newcomer, that if an issue
came up on which he had an idea he would express it. If it was a
choice between speaking up and being wrong or stepping on
somebody's toes and remaining silent and letting a good idea get
lost, he would always choose the first course. "I don't remember

having missed it," he said firmly. "If we become 'yes men,' " he thumped the table, "we will lose our freedom in no time."

Snellman has served under several ministers, including some representing the Communist Party when the Communists took part in a Left-Center coalition. "It can be very instructive to work under a Communist minister," he believes. "I was determined to support them when they did something I felt was in the national interest and the right thing for the world. If not, I would fight for my conviction, as I would under any minister." He added that the coalition government in which the Communists participated from 1978 until last year produced an economy that was regarded as exemplary by the OECD.

Snellman also mentioned an area of successful cooperation between his small country with a Western type of parliamentary democracy and a Communist superpower. "Our governments are negotiating about cooperation on environmental protection, including the reduction of acid rain which is vital for our country with 70% of its area covered by forests."

Such cooperation did not mean being naive about Communist aims. In the last forty years, he said, his country had been exposed to "every avenue of infiltration and propaganda." Yet, despite this, support for the Communists had been substantially reduced. They now had 14% of the votes in national elections. "Free people can think for themselves," he says.

Snellman, who was for five years an elder in the Helsinki Lutheran Church, said he took it for granted that any group who visited Finland from the Soviet Union came with the blessing of their government, even religious people. Orthodox Russian churchmen, for instance, would come and proclaim to "their Finnish brothers in Christ" a message of peace in identical wording to that of their political leaders. "They would do what was expected of them by the Politburo," he said. "But the Politburo can never control anyone 100%. Maybe in their hearts they have a sincere faith. It is useless to be just anti-Communist, we must try to win Communists to a superior idea."

A vital element of being a free man, he suggested, was to move from trying to stop someone else to developing a plan of your own. "It is essential to create all over the world people who have

an answer to fear and who seek God's guidance," he says.
"Human intelligence alone is inadequate for the challenge we
face."

I asked him about the issue of human rights. To speak about
human rights was important, he replied, but on one condition: that
we were totally honest about the failings of our own society.
"Otherwise," he said, "you put yourself on a pedestal of judgement and the Russians naturally don't respond."

Snellman knows the United States. America's strongest message, he insists, it that it is an open society. It admits its faults.
Like Watergate. "It is not news that we are human," he laughs, "it
is news that we are honest about it. Russia's greatest weakness is
that it can't afford to be honest. In that respect America is
superior."

The forthright Finn's parting words to me were, "Keep up your
guard but take all people to heart. Why not infiltrate the souls of
everybody, even the KGB people. Don't consider Russians are
more evil than we are."

November 15, 1984

Rajmohan Gandhi

ONE OF THE MOST INTERESTING PEOPLE I know is Rajmohan
Gandhi, a grandson of the Mahatma. I saw him recently in
Washington, DC where he is a Fellow at the Woodrow Wilson
Center for International Scholars. He, a Hindu, is researching the
lives of Muslim leaders who have influenced the history of the
subcontinent.

This is very illustrative of Gandhi's approach, the attempt to
reach out to people of different cultures and countries. "I have
had the thought," he says, "that I ought to play some part in
healing the divisions between the Hindus and Muslims, between
India and Pakistan."

Gandhi is today one of the most respected figures in India. This
respect does not stem from any position. He holds none, apart
from writing regularly in several of India's papers. It does not
stem from the family pedigree, though as well as being a grand-

son of the Mahatma he is also a grandson of C. Rajagopalachari, first Indian Governor General of independent India.

It stems, I believe, simply from his moral authority, the way he lives, and his consistent emphasis on the need in India for a revolution of character.

Gandhi gained international recognition for his courageous resistance to repression and the trampling on democratic rights in the mid-1970s when Mrs. Gandhi, no relation, locked up the opposition and censored the press. The paper which he was editing bore the full brunt of that censorship and fought its battles whenever possible in the courts. Gandhi was himself arrested. Henry Kamm, the *New York Times* Pulitzer Prize-winning journalist told me that of the people he interviewed in India at that time, Rajmohan Gandhi was about the only one who was willing to be quoted by name. Gandhi wrote in his paper at that difficult moment, "Especially when there is a climate of fear, a journalist has a duty towards his vocation, towards his conscience, towards truth, and towards his country to throw a light on injustices. How are rulers to be helped if this is not done? How do the ruled find hope if no one does it?" He went on, "Do Joan of Arc, Abraham Lincoln, and Mahatma Gandhi kindle us? They loved the constructive and the positive, but they also spoke out and struggled against the failings of rulers. Most of us will always be poor followers of these figures, but let us at least be followers."

Though he respects his grandfather's life and work, he is impatient with those who would use the Gandhi name to promote unGandhian causes. In fact, he has written, "In our foolish and selfishly motivated idolatry we are making Gandhi coins and Gandhi currency notes. These will merely add color to our corrupt monetary dealings. He used to say, 'Make God your *guru*.' If we did that instead of each one insisting on his being accepted as *guru* we would yet see a transformed India."

Of his own heritage he says, "The fact that my grandfather was a great man does not make me a good man." Indeed, as a young man he realized that if he wanted to help build a "clean, strong, and united India," as he described his aim, he would have to start by being different himself. When he contrasted his life by absolute standards of honesty, purity, unselfishness and love, he

thought immediately of some steps he should take. It can't have
been easy for someone with the Gandhi name. He describes four
of them: returning money to the Delhi Transport Undertaking for
travelling on its buses without tickets, apologizing to a friend for
jealousy because he was successful and popular, writing to his old
school principal to seek forgiveness for cheating in an examination, and being completely honest with his parents about how he
had spent his time and the money they gave him.

From such seemingly simple steps came the base for the authority he exerts today. There is a further point, he says: "It meant
also a decrease in my interest in myself and an increase in my
concern for others. Every morning it means for me a time of quiet
during which my conscience, or God's voice, can clarify my
motives and help me see where I need to change and show me
how I can change others."

Last month Gandhi spoke at a dinner in New York. His theme:
"America's role — an Asian perspective." He paid tribute to the
generosity of this country, and cited the recent decision to meet
half of Africa's need for imported food this year. He referred to
Americans who after World War II had helped Germany and its
European neighbors and Japan and its former Asian colonies to
forsake the hates of the war. He spoke of the progress made in
recent years, particularly in race relations. It was neither flawless
nor complete, he said, but one of the prouder achievements of the
country. "These are great precedents," he said, "and America is
fortunate that God enables her to count them. They offer encouragement to every American who wants to assist with a process of
reconciliation among the divided communities of our world."

Gandhi suggested that the popularity of a country was best
measured not by the words used about it at rallies or at the UN but
by the length of line of those who seek a visa to enter it. Thanks
to the Statue of Liberty, he said, many of the world's warring
communities were well represented here. "A process of reconciliation between Pakistani and Indian, Tamil and Sinhala, Sikh and
Hindu, Jew and Arab, Greek and Turk, Armenian and Turk, black
and white in South Africa," he said, "can commence on American soil."

April 4, 1985

Mary McLeod Bethune

AS BLACK HISTORY MONTH continues I'd like to talk today about a great American black educator whom I had the privilege of meeting some twenty years ago. I was interested to note that a year back, when a name was being discussed for what has since become the new Tubman Middle School in Portland her name stood high on the list. I refer to Mary McLeod Bethune.

Mrs. Bethune was born on a hot summer's day in July, 1875 in the sleepy southern hamlet of Mayesville, South Carolina. There was great excitement in the crude wooden cabin inhabited by a family of former slaves recently freed by the Emancipation Proclamation, for though she was the seventeenth child, Mary McLeod was the first one to be born free. No one could have imagined in those humble surroundings that she was destined to become one of America's most eminent educators and an advisor to two Presidents.

At an early age Mary was working with her sixteen brothers and sisters in the fields. By the time she was nine she could pick 250 pounds of cotton in a day — but she could not read or write. Education was not possible for blacks in the south in those days. Soon the church, however, began to establish mission schools, and Mary enrolled at the first to open in the area. Each day she walked five miles to school, and in the evening imparted to her family what she had learned. She worked so hard and with such faith that she became a teacher.

She opened her first school with a total capital of $1.50, and yet within ten years, starting from next to nothing, she had created a college with an enrollment of more than 600 students, the famous Bethune Cookman College in Daytona, Florida. She also found time to marry, bring up a family, become Special Advisor to Presidents Herbert Hoover and Franklin D. Roosevelt, and, over the years, to be the recipient of many honors and awards.

It was towards the end of her life, when she was eighty, that Mary McLeod Bethune encountered Moral Re-Armament. "My eyes were opened," she said at an MRA conference, "and I have seen the nations standing together regardless of race, class or color." She went on, with words which are carved on her tombstone, "To be a part of this great, uniting force of our age is the crowning experience of my life."

A successful musical, with the title, *The Crowning Experience,* was written about her, and this musical, like her life, played its part in breaking down prejudice, particularly in the southern part of the United States.

One of the most moving scenes in that film, which also happened in true life, is the apology made to Mrs. Bethune at a Moral Re-Armament conference by a white woman from Richmond, Virginia. Like Mrs. Bethune, Mrs. Sudie Wood had grown up in the south. Her grandparents had held slaves. Hers was a way of life that took for granted the customs of the past. But at that conference she had begun to face the depth of division between the races in America and how much her own feelings of superiority had contributed to that division. Sitting in a wheelchair at the back of the hall when Mrs. Bethune spoke, Mrs. Wood was very stirred. She asked her daughter to roll her to the front and there, in front of hundreds of people, she apologized humbly and sincerely for the way people like her had treated Mrs. Bethune's people.

One of the songs in *The Crowning Experience* sums up Mrs. Bethune's philosophy. It comes just before she speaks to the Washington Ladies Literary Club, the first black ever to do so: "There's always room for one more."

February 11, 1982

Our mother

THE DAY MY FATHER DIED was, my mother said later, the happiest day of her life. Let me quickly tell you that this startling remark doesn't mean what you could think it means. My parents loved each other and were happily married for thirty years. No, my mother was a woman of extraordinary faith. My father's death, at 68, was peaceful and my mother felt so borne up by faith and a certainty that this was God's plan and timing that she had an overwhelming sense that day, not of resentment and protest, but of joy and the love of God.

She was born in Dublin and named Erina. She grew up through the time of independence with machine gun fights over the roof of her house, with her school occupied by troops. Her family was everything that was unpopular — Protestant, landowner, Royal Irish Constabulary. Her father was told, "Leave Ireland by the end of the week or you will be shot," and the family home was set on fire. They moved to England where she later met and married my father, a businessman and soldier. They had two children, my brother Gerald and myself.

As World War II began it reminded my mother of the fear and death of her youth in Ireland. It looked as if England would be invaded. So my parents decided to send us to the United States for safety. When the war ended we were somewhat divided. After all, those who had survived the *Blitz,* who would jump at the sound of a slamming door, did not find it easy to communicate with children who talked about "we in America" and tended to be insensitive to what their parents had lived through in London.

It was at this point that we met Moral Re-Armament. Absolute honesty between us bridged the generation gap. My mother realized that our house was kept like a museum. "I polished the furniture and then polished off my husband when he returned," she said. It became a home. She used to smoke forty cigarettes a day. In a time of quiet reflection she thought that she should stop. For the last thirty years of her life she never touched a cigarette or wanted to. She gave up social drinking because she felt it was an area of her life where God did not have the last word.

We went as a family to the conference in Caux, Switzerland. She heard a Catholic Senator from Dublin speak. Hatred welled up in her. "Who is this lady to speak about my country when she chucked me out of it," she thought. She faced the fact that families like ours were expelled from Ireland because of the selfish way we had lived there. She apologized to the Senator and they became friends for life.

When my father died, my mother sold our home and went 'on the road,' living out of suitcases, taking the ideas that had changed her life to many places, particularly Australia, Rhodesia, as Zimbabwe was then called, and Malta. Working alongside missionaries in Rhodesia, the conviction grew that she should join the Roman Catholic Church. For someone who grew up in the Church of Ireland that was a considerable step. It was helped by her desire to work for reconciliation in Ireland.

It was typical of my mother that when she went to a well-known Jesuit center in London for instruction, she was so horrified by what she felt was the lack of moral standards and real faith, that she sought out a priest elsewhere. She was received into the Church in Switzerland and confirmed in Australia. Over the years her care had extended to people from every background all over the world. She now developed a correspondence with Archbishops, Papal Nuncios, and even the Pope. She became increasingly a force for ecumenism.

My mother did not demand that her family become Catholics but she was uncompromising in her expectation that all people, especially those of faith, live to the highest. If something was wrong she was fearless and direct in tackling it. When a relation she was staying with in Rhodesia treated his black servants badly she threatened to move out. When I had dinner alone in the apartment of a girl, my mother told me clearly that she felt it was wrong. I remember once when I was acting in a play, she came up to me afterwards and said, "You were terribly unreal all through." I said that she should tell the producer, not me. "But you *were* unreal," she insisted.

She was generous, warm-hearted, maintained the courtesies of life, letters of thanks, punctuality, and the like, had a lively Irish sense of humor and a strong belief in standards of right and wrong. Straight-backed, nearly six foot, she could be slightly forbidding as her daughters-in-law would be the first to admit. I suppose because she had faced the depth of sin in her own life, she was realistic about other people's human nature but also believed that they, like she, could find new life.

My mother developed cancer and was given only a few weeks to live. She said to a friend just before she died, "I don't think anyone enjoyed getting ready as much as I did." The Catholic priest told me, "Your mother was a toughie." I think what he meant was than even in her last days she was a considerable challenge to him.

The priest asked my mother in hospital whether she would like to make a review of her life. She replied, "No, this may sound terrible, but I am quite ready to go. I have lived my life in the light and can see myself straight." This was not pride but an assertion of the truth. As my brother commented, "She kept 'short accounts' and was up-do-date on where she needed to change."

Her last words were, "Love to everyone."

March 8, 1984

10 Principles

Opposition

Remember, remember the 5th of November,
Gunpowder, treason and plot.
I see no reason why gunpowder treason
Should ever be forgot.

THIS IS A RHYME widely known in England where they will be celebrating tonight that day nearly 400 years ago when conspirator Guy Fawkes tried unsuccessfully to blow up the British Parliament. Guy Fawkes Day, the 5th of November, is for the English a cross between Hallowe'en and the 4th of July, two days in the calendar which for some reason the English don't choose to celebrate. It's a time for fireworks and a time for children to trundle round their effigies of Guy Fawkes. Instead of "trick or treat" it's "penny for the guy"—though thanks to the ravages of inflation you wouldn't get much thanks if you gave only a penny.

All this is by way of introducing the subject of opposition in government. Some people may not go as far as Mr. Fawkes but nevertheless the way they operate in opposition could be just as destructive of democracy.

If there's one thing that makes the public cynical about politicians it is that they so often say one thing in opposition and do another when they get power. If there's one thing that makes politicians want to chuck it all in it is the selfish demands that so often meet them on all sides, in particular from people who feel that their issue or their opposing point of view is so right and so important that they are justified in overruling the democratic majority and even frustrating effective government.

Politics needn't be that way and I want to tell you about a different kind of politician who recently visited Portland. He is Kim Beazley from Australia who was the youngest member of his country's Parliament when he started and the longest-serving, 32 years, when he retired, a political figure who has been described as one of the finest men in public life Australia has ever had.

As a young politician Beazley faced the question: was he to use the issues in his country to advance his own public standing or was he to use his time and energies in the cause of bringing healing to public life? He chose the latter course. He also had the promise, he said, that if he lived straight, then God would use him to work effectively for the welfare of the Aborigine people.

For 23 years he was in opposition from 1949 to 1972. Yet it was from the Opposition benches that he achieved great gains for the country. Indeed when he was given a doctorate by the Australian National University, the citation pointed out that his two great achievements—the healing of the ulcer of sectarian bitterness in education and the enhancement of the dignity of the Aborigine people — came because he had worked irrespective of party political gain. In those years in Opposition, Beazley said, he had come to the conclusion that the true function of an opposition was to out-think the government at the point of its successes. Only then could alternative competitive policies be framed and social advance take place. "If my motive is simply power," he once said, "I will look for ways to be destructive, to eliminate those who stand in the way by defamation, and defamation in politics is the certain sign of a motive not of service but for power."

Of course, when he later became Minister for Education he was also able to initiate significant legislation that transformed Aborigine educational opportunities.

Beazley did not get defensive when his or his party's or his country's shortcomings were pointed out for he was committed to remedying them. For instance, when he was Chairman of the Parliamentary Committee on Human Rights in the Soviet Union, the Soviet Ambassador protested about the existence of the Committee. An embassy spokesman said that if Australia persisted in investigating the Soviet Union then the Soviet Union would investigate the plight of the Aborigines. Beazley immediately welcomed the suggestion on behalf of his committee pointing out that Australia like the Soviet Union was a signatory of the Helsinki accord on human rights. Therefore he would welcome a searchlight being trained on the problem. It would help them come to grips with it.

What was it that gave Beazley the perspective to continue so many years along this line, even to the point that he was willing to sacrifice the chance to be prime minister? The Melbourne University Press in some educational studies published last year devotes a chapter to Beazley's government experience. In it Beazley gives a clue: "On assuming the portfolio of education I followed the practice of taking the first hour of the morning between 6 am and 7 am to think about the problems of the portfolio, to write down what I felt needed to be done, and in conscience to eliminate motives of spite, self-defence, resentment, self-interest and the using of people. In politics there are always efforts to defeat others in party selection ballots, to discredit others, and of course to defeat sitting members in elections. The mechanisms of self-defence one develops are the antithesis of the creative thinking necessary for first class administration, and I found the practice of an hour's thought a way to escape self-centeredness."

So perhaps if you are tempted, like Guy Fawkes, to put a bomb under politicians, just remember Kim Beazley. You might even consider also whether you are ready to accept in your own life those qualities of selflessness you so desire in those elected to represent you.

November 5, 1981

Use of time

I WANT TO TALK today about time — not the news magazine but that precious commodity we never seem to have enough of.

Last week I read in the papers two astonishing news items — one about a time frame so inconceivably small, and the other about a concept of space so immeasurably large that I find it hard to take them in. The first item, apparently a fact, is that Bell Laboratories have developed a flash of light that lasts thirty millionths of a billionth of a second. That is just enough time to allow light to travel one-third the thickness of a hair on my head. The second item, still in the realm of conjecture, is that a Seattle professor believes there may be as many as ten million civilizations with our level of intelligence among the hundred billion stars in the Milky Way galaxy.

Whether there is anything in this or not, one is reminded of what the 17th century English writer and author, Sir Thomas Browne, said, "The created world is but a small parenthesis in eternity."

We do indeed live in a paradoxical situation. On the one hand eternity, on the other our very finite individual existence which we want to have count for something. Of course, whatever perspective you take there is one inescapable fact: you will be older at the end of my talk than you were at the beginning!

Here in our developed western society we are run by the clock, the digital clock. When you invite people for dinner you expect them at the agreed hour. When you have an appointment you by and large expect to be there on time.

If you have ever lived in the east you will know that people there have a much more relaxed view of time. Now, obviously we can't transplant an eastern sense of time on western society. But can we all the same be liberated from some of the worst expressions of "big clock is watching you?"

Can our political leaders, business leaders, community leaders be freed from the pressure of time. They sometimes have calendars so full you can't see them for months, and they are lucky if they ever have unhurried time with their families, let alone the space necessary to get an over-view on current events and on the future.

An Asian friend of mine was in Washington some time back. He said to a well-known political figure, "Senator, I have the feeling that the future of democracy may depend on the willingness of some Senators and Congressmen to hang a 'Do Not Disturb' notice on their doors."

A German politician was suffering under this burden of over-busyness. His health and his family life were assailed by a relentless workload, a round of meetings, speeches, campaign trips. He was, however, a man of faith and he took some time to seek inspiration on what should be done about his parliamentary schedule. He had three very simple thoughts: "1) There are things you are doing that other members could do better. Let them do them. 2) There are things you are doing well but that other younger members should be given the chance to do. Give them that chance. 3) There are things you are doing out of ambition and fear of defeat at the polls that do not need to be done at all. Stop doing them." He acted on these thoughts and became a free man. Not only did he find time to think and to be with his family, but also each day to have at least one personal talk with a fellow member of parliament.

Of course, you don't have to be a politician to have an over-crowded day. I sometimes find it myself. I have come to the conclusion that a full calendar is not necessarily a bad thing. What is bad is when your own temperament or your health is affected by it, when the completion of a job becomes more important than consideration for those you are working with, when the pressure of deadlines makes you irritable or short with others, when your week days and your weekends become inseparable to the exclusion of your family.

I have what some may regard as a rather simplistic philosophy, that is that at any given moment there is only one thing I am meant to be doing and that whatever it is I should put my whole heart into it. So the basic issue is to be sure that you are doing what you are meant to be doing. The problem emerges or is cured in your motives and the way in which you plan your day.

I have a simple recipe which I recommend from thirty years' practice. I get up earlier than I need to each day to take time to get perspective on my motives and the program ahead. I subscribe to the view of St. Francis of Sales who said that a half hour in quiet is an indispensable way to start the day. Unless you are exceptionally busy. Then a whole hour is better.

Just one footnote on time. This weekend we have to change our clocks. If you can't remember which way, here is a helpful tip to remember: spring forward, fall back. Spring forward, fall back. By the way, I think it is the one occasion where you can lose an hour and not be any older. Have a good time.

April 22, 1982

Honesty

THE HORRORS of World War II were evoked and memories in part healed at a dramatic occasion in Portland in July. I mention it now as the event to which I refer was overlooked by the press, although sensitively described on one TV channel. I was particularly alert to it as it involved a German visitor who was staying in our home.

Peter Petersen, a senior member of the Federal German Parliament and the ranking member of his country's Armed Services Committee, was speaking to the City Club at a lunch cosponsored by the World Affairs Council.

The audience of more than two hundred had responded warmly to his forthright presentation of his government's policies and his ringing affirmation of faith in the United States when an elderly Jewish gentleman rose to ask a question.

There was consternation as he demanded that the speaker say whether he had been a Nazi or not. "Tension rippled through the group," a TV reporter said on the news later. It was certainly true. Some in the audience wanted to hush the questioner. Some felt the speaker need not respond. But the visiting German politician wanted to.

"I was an enthusiastic Hitler Youth boy," said Peter Petersen, adding that he would have become a Party member if he had not been too young when drafted into the army. "In 1945 I thought the fact that the Americans and Russians had won the war only proved that they had more guns and bombs. It did not affect my conviction that Hitler was right and everybody else wrong."

A few months later, after escaping from a British prison camp, he had met for the first time in his own home a Jew who had survived eight years in concentration camps. "He, without blaming me personally," said Petersen, "told me his story. Until then, I thought all the concentration camp news was British propaganda."

That night Petersen could not sleep. He wanted to emigrate to Australia so that he could forget that he was a German. He was persuaded by his father to remain. "You stay right here," his father had said. "It was easy for you to follow the flag then but now your country needs you more."

At that point, said the German visitor, he had fallen into the trap into which millions of his generation had fallen, of working to prove that he was better than all the Germans who were in the S.S. or running the concentration camps.

In 1947 he had met Christian friends who had helped him rethink his life. Suddenly he remembered something which had happened to him two years before in Silesia. He had been watching a group of people in terrible shape, heavily guarded by the S.S., being herded from one cattle car to another. He had asked his lieutenant who they were. The officer replied, "Oh, don't worry, they are just Poles and Jews."

"The terrible thing," the German politician told the City Club, "was that I did not worry, because that reason was good enough for me. And I realized the moral insensitivity which made Hitler possible was as much part of me as it was of these S.S. people. Only by the grace of God I was not in the S.S."

Petersen said that after he had told this experience in a more detailed way to his Christian friends he had realized what forgiveness meant not just for himself personally but also as a German. "Since that day I am free," he said.

Those who were present at this re-living of a frightening period in world history, said Chuck Dimond on KOIN-TV, "are not likely to forget about it any time soon."

Sitting alone in the Benson Hotel ballroom, Dimond concluded his account of the occasion with these words: "The meeting room where Peter Petersen offered his chilling revelation is now empty. But the echoes continue, of his admonition, his plea that it not happen again, of the standing ovation that followed. But even more there is an echo from perhaps his most constructive confession — 'And I realized the moral insensitivity which made Hitler possible was as much part of me as it was of these S.S. people. Only by the grace of God I was not in the S.S.' "

Peter Petersen understands the need for the Jewish people to keep Holocaust alive in the memory of people to prevent a second one. But Hitler has been dead for 35 years, he points out, and Nazism does not stand a chance in his country. What is important now is to apply the lessons of yesterday to the threats of today.

Writing in the newspaper of his part of Germany, the *Stuttgarter Zeitung,* he states, "If we Germans are to derive any lesson out of the Hitler time, then it is that we may never again look the other way whenever helpless people suffer through the actions of other people or states."

That, like his honesty at the City Club, is a challenge to all of us.

August 18, 1983

Quiet

IT'S OFFICIAL. It will probably soon be taught in management schools. It has even got an acronym by which to recognize it. Something which I and my friends have been experimenting with for years in secret is now coming into the open and has been given the ultimate accolade in twentieth century America—corporate approval.

I refer to the habit, honed through centuries of research and application, of commencing each day with an hour in quiet.

There it was staring at me in cold print, an Associated Press dispatch from Bakersfield, California. The Western Region Headquarters of the Continental Telephone Company has set aside a quiet hour from 8 to 9 for its accounting staff to address long-term projects, research, reports, or other creative work that requires concentration. This quiet hour, the dispatch goes on, is especially designed for those who work in open plan offices and has been designated AMP—achieving maximum potential.

During the hour set aside at the telephone company the accounting staff do not participate in meetings, run errands, or engage in other distracting activities, and only emergency phone calls are accepted. "It's like an invisible force field we can create to allow us one hour of quiet time," says the staff manager. One supervisor said that before the advent of AMP he had never had time to get important things done. Another is quoted by the Associated Press as saying that now they made a game of seeing how much they could get done in an hour. "I had one project on the back burner for several months," he says, "and I was able to complete it in seven hours."

I am sure that when the obvious productivity benefits of a quiet time become more widely known the practice will spread beyond the open plan of the accounting department and the board room of the Continental Telephone Company. Who knows, AMP might become so fashionable that workers would continue it on Saturdays and Sundays at home and through their vacations. This addiction might spread to whole families.

An independent researcher two hundred years ago also stumbled on this early morning practice. He is the English statesman and man of letters, Lord Chesterfield. It was he who said "Whatever is worth doing at all, is worth doing well" and "Never put off till tomorrow what you can do today." Despite the fact that he also said "Advice is seldom welcome, and those who want it the most always like it the least" let me pass on his endorsement of this quiet hour. It is from a letter to a friend: "One method more I recommend to you by which I have found great benefit, even in the most dissipated part of my life, that is to rise early, and at the same hour every morning, how late whatsoever you may have sat up the night before. This secures you an hour or two, at least, of reading and reflection, before the common interruptions of the morning begin; and it will save your constitution, by forcing you to go to bed early, at least one night in three. It will procure you both more time and more taste for your pleasures; and so far from being troublesome to you, that, after you have pursued it a month, it would be troublesome to you to lay it aside."

Of course, the wise Lord carries the Bakersfield concept further. His advice invokes the discipline of early rising — and you don't get paid to do it like the phone people. As a practitioner of many years standing I can attest that it is a worthwhile pursuit. It offers an uninterrupted time of reflection where you clear away the debris of the day before and sort out the priorities of the day ahead. And there is even a further dimension to it. It could be the chance to tap into a bank of wisdom which if acted on can be time-saving, stress-shedding and problem-disentangling. I mean the wisdom of an even wiser Lord. Père Gratry, a French priest in the last century, wrote, "As the sun is always shining so God is constantly speaking. How do you listen to God? The best time is in the morning before all distractions and activities intervene. How can you listen to God, you ask me? This is the answer: you write. Write so that you may better hear that word that is in you and keep His instructions."

Peter Howard, a great English journalist with whom I worked, put that experience this way, "As I begin each day by listening to God, it is a time of enthralment and fascination that I would not miss. It is like a great shoal of silver fish flashing through your heart and mind — new ideas for people, fresh approaches to problems, deeper insight into the mood of the times, costly, daily, personal decision that is the price of shifting our nation ahead. I am not much of a fisherman but I try and snatch one or two of those silvery fish as they fly from the mind of God into the mind of men and women and children like ourselves."

It is a long way from the back burners of Bakersfield to the silver fish of Howard. A quiet time is the common component. If we, too, begin each day with those sixty uninterrupted minutes who knows where that may lead us, perhaps to, what was it, AMP, achieving maximum potential.

January 31, 1985

Expectations

I MEET PEOPLE who swear by Reagan. They hang on his every word. They underline his speeches. They see him through rose-tinted spectacles. They rejoice at the discomfiture of his opponents.

Then I meet others, many others, who swear at Reagan, who haven't a good word for him, who see red at his policies, whose conversation seems like one long moan of blame.

I don't find either approach particularly helpful or uplifting. Modern government is so huge and the issues facing our leaders so complex that they need alongside them those who will speak the truth with compassion rather than sycophants or gravediggers.

I was talking with a professional actor in London one day. He was understudying a main role on the West End stage, a role that was being extraordinarily well played. I said to him, "You must be very torn between wanting the success of the play and wanting the actor to drop dead." "I'm not torn at all," he replied. "I wish he'd drop dead."

Sometimes our approach to government seems to be along these lines. We have little compassion or understanding for those who are entrusted with authority. Our point of view, sometimes our advancement, are all that matters to us. Like my actor friend we are consumed by the belief that we will do it better and sometimes forget that more is at stake than our political ambitions or the chip on our shoulder.

Of course I am not just talking about presidential and national affairs. The same weaknesses are apparent at a humbler level. We tend to see people as they are. We like or we dislike them. We approve or disapprove their policies. Seldom does it cross our minds that we could live in a way and even speak in a way that helps them to be different.

A Greek friend of mine whose husband was British — they didn't always find it the easiest thing to get along—once gave me a good recipe for family life. "I think I am meant to love Peter as he is," she said, "but fight for him to be what he is meant to be." We are sometimes so busy scheming to replace people or frustrate their plans that we don't work to help them to be what they are meant to be or help them to formulate plans that are better—let alone love them.

I was present more than thirty years ago when a wise American, Frank Buchman, spoke these words: "Party lines don't hold the way they used to. Democrats and Republicans, it doesn't seem to make much difference. Some are good and some — not so good. But what is so hard to find is the leadership, the type of man to be in Washington, the universal type of man that really meets people's deepest needs. There are so few in whom the people place their full confidence. It used to be a fairly easy job to be in Washington, wrought with honour. But now with the divergent views it is beginning to be a considerable nuisance, unless a man has the art of giving something everybody wants."

If we're going to help create that universal type of man or

woman for Washington, we may have to become more universal type of people ourselves here at home. What does that mean?

First of all I believe it means being willing sometimes to listen before we put forward our views. I remember an Australian bishop in Papua New Guinea telling me how he used to have to be ready to sit in a meeting with Papuans for an hour with nobody saying anything, all the while by training and experience wanting to jump in and break the silence, to keep quiet until the Papuans spoke first, otherwise they would never speak. It may also be a question of being willing to listen after we have spoken. I heard this week of a US ambassador who was intending to present Reagan's views at an international conference and then leave. It was suggested that it would do more for America if the ambassador stayed on to listen to what other nations had to say.

It means, too, that we are not so set in our opinions that we cannot keep our links of friendship with everyone. I may feel strongly as an Englishman that Britain was right to react with force in the South Atlantic but if I meet an Argentinian it may be more productive to tell him how sorry I am for the insensitivity we have shown to his country and its people's feelings over many years.

We must keep open channels of communication rather than getting drawn into making false choices. For instance, pro Israel or pro PLO — when it is possible to see the justice and the weakness in the action of both communities; pro one man one vote or pro apartheid in South Africa—when one can be for neither and be pro change in black and white; pro nuclear freeze or pro nuclear war— when you can honorably be anti both.

In all these conflict areas people are needed who can see the situation from the other side of the hill and, if they have views, can put them forward firmly but humbly without belligerence.

Finally, we need to have the expectation that people can change their views, that time or age, mood or maturity, rational discussion or even moral and spiritual experience can change the furniture of a person's mind and temper attitudes of a lifetime. So never assume that someone else is any less open to new ideas than we are. Or are we?

June 24, 1982

Sportsmanship

TWO STORIES about sports caught my eye recently. One was quoting Cathy Rigby, the gymnast, on her view that parents often pushed their children too much. The other was about tennis star, Ivan Lendl, from Czechoslovakia, who earned more than two million dollars last year but is under investigation for taking prohibited payments. I noted also that he has been suspended from an important European tournament for shouting obscenities.

There may be no connection between Cathy Rigby's words and Ivan Lendl's actions, but as we have an eleven-year-old daughter, Juliet, who is very keen on sports, we are also interested in learning how to encourage her enthusiasms without getting things out of perspective. Her last year's ambition has at least been frustrated. She wanted to be the first woman to play on the Timbers soccer team, now disbanded.

Sports have always played a big part in my life since at about the age of five I went to bed with my first soccer boots. I went to a high school in England where participation in organized sports was compulsory. Whether you liked it or not, whether you were good at it or not, rain or shine, you played or else. Some of us were so keen that the school had to forbid organized sport on Sundays. The school spirit was built around the playing of rugby. In fact, most boys put the captain of rugby on a far higher pedestal than the winner of a scholarship to Oxford. I can still recite a description of the cap awarded to those who got what here would be called their rugby letter: chocolate velvet divided into eight equal parts by vertical silver lines, silver monogram on peak, silver tassel. If, as a first year boy, I didn't know things like that and couldn't name all fifteen members of the school's rugby team with their initials, then I would be beaten. Attendance at home games played by the team against other schools was also compulsory. Even the masters, the teachers, had to raise a team to play against the school.

Now all of this is, of course, a bit out of proportion and must have been agony for some people. But on the whole I think that the lessons learned from sport, particularly team sport, are salutary, not to mention the gain in fitness that comes from playing rather than applauding or discussing sport. I have a feeling that if more people played and played longer, there wouldn't have to be so many people jogging with such pained expressions on our highways and byways. One English newspaper, commenting on this devotion to physical fitness in America, described it as "a cross between joggers anonymous and Moral Re-Armament."

Despite that initial school experience, or perhaps because of it, I love playing games. I was once asked what my idea of heaven would be and I replied 'a perpetual game.' I have had the good fortune as I grew up for a time in America to have played both American and English games in interschool competition — rugby and football, cricket and baseball, field hockey and ice hockey. I've had the chance to sail in Nigeria, to bowl in Japan, to play cricket in Kenya, to play table tennis on the Atlantic, even to play golf in the Himalayas. And I'm lucky to be still playing ice hockey, soccer and tennis in Portland.

If there's one thing sport does it is to show you your real nature. I may think I'm a peace-loving sort of chap who doesn't get easily riled, who doesn't retaliate. A hard game of soccer tells me it's just not true. I may not trip an opponent deliberately, I may bite off the rude word I feel like saying, my querying of the referee may be hushed, but it doesn't disguise from me what I'm like underneath. And that's healthy. I may say the same thing applies when I'm supporting my daughter's basketball or soccer team.

She gave me a poster that's appropriate. It is of Snoopy dressed for tennis. Snoopy says, "It doesn't matter if you win or lose — until you lose." Winning, I suppose because of the rewards, has become too important.

Two psychologists at the University of California have suggested that athletic violence is related to moral development and that the tough guys on the field are not morally mature. It would be interesting if they also turned their attention to the spectators as well as the players. I was brought up in the school where you didn't question a referee's or umpire's decision. It was right once it had been made. Instant replays unfortunately feed the idea that one should question a referee's judgement. I had to referee an indoor soccer game last week. My biggest headache was parents trying to get me to penalize illegal use of hands which I didn't see and even declare a goal which I didn't think was one.

As I said, sports show up my true nature. But I don't have to be run by it. Every time a player gives in to his nature or commits what has come to be called a professional foul, it contributes to the decline in society. For so many millions take their cues from sportsmen, follow their values. Every time a sportsman is what used to be called sportsmanlike he adds to everyone's faith. Like the ice hockey player who last year refused the instructions of his coach to join a fight on the ice. Or Swedish tennis star Mats Wilander who at set point in the semi-final of the French Open Championships gave his opponent a chance to replay a point because he had disputed the line call. Or Bobby Jones, who some think the best golfer of all time, who once drove a ball into the wood, just touched it, declared it—and lost a tournament. When praised for this, he said, "You might as well praise a man for not robbing a bank."

I would truly prefer that our daughter played the game in that spirit than won any medals. I'd like to do the same myself. Is that old-fashioned? Or is that perhaps the new fashion we need if society is to survive?

May 26, 1983

How we treat others

WE ARE DRAWING to the end of what is designated Black History month. It has been a time when, if one's ears are open, one may have heard things said which, for those of us who are white at least, are hard to accept. That is natural. It is shameful the way black people have been treated by whites for centuries, and are still treated in many cases, and the way history too has been distorted. If sometimes we feel that there is over-reaction or exaggeration then we must remember that, as in the situation in Northern Ireland, feelings are facts which must be taken into account if we are going to learn to live together.

Conrad Hunte, a courageous West Indian sportsman, spoke in Portland last year and expressed the view that those who have suffered most have the most to give the modern world. He went so far as to suggest that only through a willingness on the part of blacks to give in that dimension could some white people be helped to face up to their own need to be radically different. Such an approach seems to me to bear a distinct kinship with that of Mahatma Gandhi. As one person said to me who saw the film about Gandhi the other day, "He wanted to shame the British into change."

This valiant view of life brings to mind the experiences of two friends of mine, one black, the other white. The black man is Richard Brown whom I first met thirty years ago when we acted together in a stage play and about whom Conrad Hunte spoke when he addressed a Portland conference last year. Hunte said that Brown's story answered two important questions: how do you talk to someone who won't listen to you and how do you love someone who won't let you love them?

In 1954 as a result of the Supreme Court decision in the case of Brown versus the Board of Education all American schools were supposed to be desegregated. Professor Richard Brown was teaching at Bluefield State College in West Virginia. As a result of that ruling, Bluefield State, which up to that point had been an all black college, became predominantly white, both in its faculty and in its student body. Dr. Brown who was Dean found himself number two to a white president. Most staff and students accepted the position except for three white professors who made life hell for Brown.

Now, the Dean had committed himself to a policy of caring for everyone equally as best he could but, as he said, these folks wouldn't let him love them. And after a while he began to hate them passionately. One morning, taking a time of quiet reflection he had the thought, "You can't always decide how you feel about people but you can decide how you treat them. Treat them as though they were your best friends, so that anyone looking on would think they were your brothers." "I certainly didn't feel that way," he said, "but at least I could try."

For the next while he worked on these inner guidelines. One of the whites was Brown's deputy in math and chemistry. After a few months he came to Brown and said, "I notice you have been very busy of late so I have worked out the schedule for math and chemistry for the next semester." The men began to talk and remained friends and brothers until Brown's death. Then a little later the second professor came to him and told him that one of his family was in trouble and that he was the only person he felt he could talk to about it. They talked and, as Conrad Hunte said, they became brothers. The third man took a little longer but he, too, by the end of the year had a reconciliation with Brown. Together they began to make Bluefield State a pattern of voluntary desegregation. For this, Professor Brown was honored by his City Council.

The second experience is from the continent of Africa. It is that of Agnes Hofmeyr, who is one of the Leakey family of Kenya. Agnes's father, Gray Leakey, was a much respected white man in Kenya. He spoke Kikuyu fluently. The Kikuyu tribe honored him with a name in their own language "Morungaru," which means tall and upright. But a Kikuyu prophetess had said that if a good white man were offered as a sacrifice to the gods of Mount Kenya it would restore the failing fortunes of Mau Mau.

So sixty Mau Mau broke into the family farm, killed Agnes' stepmother and carried her father up the slopes of Mount Kenya where they buried him alive as a human sacrifice. When she heard the news Agnes declared, "I say 'no' to bitterness and the desire for revenge." In the next years she and her husband continued to work for the growth in character and compassion of people of all races all over the world and in South Africa where they live.

Two years ago Agnes met face to face one of the revolutionary council who decided that her father should be killed. He apologized for what was done to her father. Agnes responded by recommitting herself to work even harder for an answer to division, and for the change in black and white.

None of us has any choice what color we are. None of us is to blame for what happened before we were born. But we are all responsible for the way we treat each other now and, if we so choose, we can also accept responsibility for the way people like us treated other people in the past. Richard Brown and Agnes Hofmeyr are a challenge to all of us whatever our race.

It was Martin Luther King, who drew inspiration from Mahatma Gandhi, who said, "Unearned suffering is redemptive." When he accepted the Nobel Peace Prize, he said, "Man must evolve for all human conflict a method which rejects revenge, aggression and retaliation."

February 24, 1983

Moral Re-Armament

I AM INTRODUCED each week as someone from Moral Re-Armament. What, indeed, is Moral Re-Armament? I was asked this week to answer that question at a public occasion in the city. This is what I said.

Our world is not made up basically of goodies and baddies. Though it would be convenient to think so. Our world is made up of people like you and me and the line between good and bad is a shifting line that goes through each one of our hearts and lives each day. That is why we need an answer more fundamental than blame. All of us can think of some other person or some other group that needs to be different. We blame the other member of the family, the other political party, the other race, the other denomination, the other religion. We blame our government, we blame foreign governments, we blame the system, we even blame society.

Moral Re-Armament says very simply: if you want to see the world different, the most practical place to start is with yourself, your group, your nation. When you point your finger at your neighbor there are three more pointing back at you. And once you have started with yourself you begin to get insights that will help others change.

That change in people, Moral Re-Armament believes, is the key to a new society. Change in government, new organizations, different structures have their part. But how often today's radicals have become tomorrow's reactionaries because in their enthusiasm and passion they did not remember that unless you deal with selfishness you only replace one lot of selfish rulers with another. We need new men and women if we are going to build a better future. We need different men and women if we are going to have peace.

I have a good friend who was in on the founding of the United Nations, who has been in diplomacy all his life and more recently has been working with the Brandt Commission. The problems on the conference table are immense, he says, but often so are the problems sitting round the table and no one is dealing with them. The human factor, he believes, is not only the forgotten factor but often also the decisive one.

Let me tell you about another friend of mine, Lionel Jardine, who was a senior British administrator in pre-independence India. He was aloof and a walking example of that saying, "You can tell an Englishman anywhere but you cannot tell him much." He came home on leave to England. He was worn out by efforts to bring law and order in the Northwest Frontier Province and thinking of resigning. He met Frank Buchman, the initiator of Moral Re-Armament, who challenged him to go back to India and live differently.

Jardine decided to do so. Back in the Northwest Frontier Province the change was evident. For he wrote letters of apology to an Indian colleague and to two Indian lawyers to whom he had been rude. Before long as many as fifty people of all backgrounds would meet in the Jardine's home to plan for the welfare of the community. The leader of the Nationalist Party commented later, "Mr. Jardine's change of heart was perceptibly noticeable. From being an absolute autocrat he became an actual servant of the people." And the chief minister said, "We have had two Lionel Jardines here. One before change, the other after. Of the former we will not speak. Of the latter we cannot have too much."

News reached Mahatma Gandhi of the change in Jardine and others and the fact that as a result the Northwest Frontier had become the one area without disturbances in the country. He had it investigated and found it was true. "Politics has become like a great game of chess," said Gandhi. "Both sides know the value of the pieces and the moves to make. But when men's motives and aims are changed, like these have been, the chessboard is upset and we can begin again."

That is what Moral Re-Armament is about — upsetting the board and starting again in any situation because people's motives have changed.

It is not an organization which you join. There are no members, no dues. No one gets paid. It is a way of life. It is not a spare time activity but what you decide to live for twenty-four hours a day.

To focus where change is needed in each of us Moral Re-Armament insists on the need for absolute moral standards of honesty, purity, unselfishness and love. Facing those standards in our own lives is where each one of us can begin. It may require restitution. The standards become yardsticks for private and public life.

To give direction to this work we depend on taking time in quiet. I get up an hour earlier every morning. I write down my thoughts. I test them against those standards. I act on them. For those who think in such terms it is handing over your life to God for him to guide you. For those who don't it is being true to the deepest prompting of your heart.

For more than fifty years now men and women of all backgrounds have been living this way, working together intelligently and globally, and the fruit has been the resolving of disputes in family, in industry, in the nation and sometimes between nations.

All of us here know places where we are not living as we should, resolutions we have not kept, places where we have cut corners we should not have cut. As we decide today to do something about those things in our lives we are immediately part of the Moral Re-Armament of the world.

January 27, 1983